SHE'S
SO
BOSS

SHE'S SO BOSS

THE GIRL ENTREPRENEUR'S GUIDE TO
IMAGINING, CREATING & KICKING ASS

STACY KRAVETZ

Quercus

Quercus

New York · London

© 2017 by Stacy Kravetz

First published in the United States by Quercus in 2017

ISBN 9781681444161

Library of Congress Control Number: 2016962836

Distributed in the United States and Canada by
Hachette Book Group
1290 Avenue of the Americas
New York, NY 10104

This publication is designed to provide competent and reliable information regarding the subject matter covered. However, it is sold with the understanding that the author and publisher are not engaged in rendering legal, financial, or other professional advice. Laws and practices often vary from state to state and if legal or other expert assistance is required, the services of a professional should be sought. The author and publisher specifically disclaim any liability that is incurred from the use or application o the contents of this book.

Printed in Canada

2 4 6 8 10 9 7 5 3 1

www.quercus.com

To my soul sisters, the Westlake School for Girls class of '86.

ACKNOWLEDGMENTS

Thank you to the bosses who paved the way and to those who bust the glass ceiling daily.

Thank you to the many people who contributed in ways great and small to this book: Nathaniel Marunas, for believing in this project on description. Amelia Ayrelan Iuvino, for your patience and expertise. You've made this book better with every edit. Sharyn Rosart and Lynne Yeamans, for your design skill and artful eye. Adrienne Becker, Boss role model and partner in crime. I'm indebted to Niharika Bedekar, Chental-Song Bembry, Deepika Bodapati, Juliette Brindak Blake, Alexandra Douwes, The Fe Maidens, Debbie Fung, Allyson Greenfield, Priscilla Guo, Gabrielle Jordan, Neeka Mashouf, Nellie Morris, Naama Raz-Yaseef, and Chelsea Siler.

Jesse and Oliver, thanks for being patient. The next book will be for boys. And to Jay, thank you for listening and for always having my back.

CONTENTS

FOREWORD

BY JACKIE EMERSON

'm Jackie. I am an actress, I am a singer, I am a student, I am a creator, I am a businesswoman, and I am carving my own path. I wear Gryffindor socks. I like funny hats. I am on my school's improv team (which means I embarrass myself almost constantly). I dance wildly in cars. I sing everywhere I go. And I want to change the world.

I also get extremely insecure. I've overcome terrible stage fright. I've battled disordered eating, and I still grapple with my body image. I used to worry my friends were talking about me behind my back. At a university that attracts brilliant students from all over the world, I often feel like I might not be smart enough. I sometimes get exceedingly lonely.

Over time, I've realized that these things that are supposed weaknesses, imperfections, and vulnerabilities actually make me stronger, because they make me who I am, and I have finally come to a place where I am not afraid of that—most of the time. There are some days when I feel much more comfortable with myself than others, but I also recognize that ups and downs are a part of the journey.

I didn't realize I had disordered eating until I was onstage in front of 300 people, talking about what it means to have a healthy body image. I was using buzzwords like "self-confidence" and "empowerment" when an audience member asked me a question about my own daily practices in self-love, and I was painfully hit with the realization that I didn't actually love myself—at least not physically.

I began to open up to these strangers about my own experience, my own journey with my body and food and family and media. I started crying. Then, to my surprise, a girl from the audience stood up and began sharing her story. Then another, and another. This panel on healthy body image became a group therapy session of sorts. And I have never felt as much love and support and togetherness as I felt in that room.

After that experience, I began to do this talk in many different places, at conventions and schools. I started an online web series called "Let's Get Real": a forum to openly discuss some of the most difficult issues we deal with, including mental health, body image, sexual orientation, cyberbullying, and anything else participants wanted to discuss. Though it may not be my most-viewed work by commercial standards, it's one of the things I'm proudest of creating. If we can come together and support each other in meaningful ways, each one of us becomes stronger and more likely to thrive and succeed.

People of every color, people of every identity, people with every experience, should grow up in a world where they are encouraged to open any door and step right in, be it the computer science lab, the CEO's office, or the director's seat. We must dare to dream of new possibilities, new ideas and innovations, and we must believe we can do anything we set our minds to. And we deserve to have the resources and support that we need to pursue those dreams in a tangible way.

Today women have many more opportunities than they used to have. We should be proud of that legacy, and proud of the women who fought for those rights and blazed new trails ahead of us. Nonetheless, we have so much further to go, and so much more to fight for.

Taking a risk is scary. Following dreams can often put you in a very vulnerable position. But you do it because you can't imagine not doing it, whether you are starting a business or forming a band or launching a nonprofit or painting or cooking or running for office. You do it because it is in your breath and blood and bones and soul, and you know that if you don't take a chance, you'll never turn your dreams into reality.

This is what it means to be a boss—to do that scary thing, regardless of the challenges and despite the risks. By working to bring something new to this world, you are guaranteed to change it in some small way. And maybe even in a big way.

If you have an idea for something you want to see on this planet, though, chances are you don't have the knowledge and skills yet to transform your vision into action. And that's okay—some things, especially in the business world, simply have to be learned. Young women specifically sometimes need a boost in that arena, because a lot of the information out there about pursuing success or starting a business isn't aimed toward us.

That's where *She's So Boss* comes in.

This book contains stories and tools that will help you find your inner boss and encourage the confidence and leadership potential that already exist in you. Your inner boss encompasses not just the uniquely wonderful skills you possess but also the flaws that make you who you are. Insecurities and vulnerabilities may actually be your greatest form of strength. Own them. Take them on your journey.

I believe in many things, but above all, I believe in the power of a girl who believes in herself.

So no matter what anyone tries to tell you along the way, always remember this: You are boss.

INTRODUCTION

Always think big. Especially in the face of those who tell you to scale it back, tone it down, think just a tiny bit smaller. Yes, especially then. When you get into business, whether at age 10 or at age 25, you will come across people who will try, sometimes in a well-intentioned way, to modify your dreams. They will tell you to aim lower so you'll be more apt to hit your mark. They may warn you that what you're trying to do is going to be really, really hard. Or even impossible. They're not doing it to be mean. They're thinking about you and your fragile little heart, worrying that you'll shoot for the moon and then give up if you can't get there. So don't be too mad at them. Just listen and nod your head and say thank you. You should always be polite, especially when someone's doling out free advice. But then walk away with a secret smile on your face because you know something they don't: you're a badass boss. And when you hear something negative, you hear challenge.

When you talk about your dreams of running a business, from concept to execution, you should always **THINK BIG**. To achieve something big you need to conceptualize it. You need to strive and plan and hope and plan some more. It takes work, but you're up to the challenge. Just set your compass in the direction you intend to go. In the nitty-gritty world of making your business happen day-to-day, there will be opportunities to reconsider, reframe, and retool. But never stop aiming high or thinking big.

BEING BOSS

WHEN YOU'RE IN CHARGE, YOU RUN THE SHOW. Being "boss" means being *the* boss, acting as a benevolent captain of your own ship, which will sail wherever you point it. You are in charge of yourself and anyone else who works for you and with you to achieve your business goals.

Good bosses lead by example, which means you are the face of your business. Take a good, hard look at your number one employee—*you*—and make sure she's doing a good job. Be the kind of boss you'd like to work for.

There's also the less tangible concept of being "Boss." It's all about attitude. Women who are Boss don't have to run businesses, though many of them do. Some are women you've heard of and others you'll wish you had. Whether it was Nellie Bly, digging up newspaper stories in the nineteenth century, or Beyoncé, rocking out with cut-to-the-point lyrics today, there's no shortage of Boss women who are leading the way. And there's no reason why you shouldn't be one of them. There is room for all of us.

BOSS IS A STATE OF MIND. A Boss is a take-charge chick with big ideas and limitless ambitions. Boss is the way you see yourself and the way you project yourself to the world. To be Boss is to be your own brand of hip, cool, and awesome, to define yourself the way you want to be—whether that's quietly confident, loud and take-charge, or mad creative—it's you. You're it. You're the business. Success or failure, no one can take your Boss-ness away from you.

THE STARTING POINT IS ATTITUDE. In order to be a Boss, you must have confidence in yourself. Not everything you do will be perfect, but as long as you believe in yourself, you know that you'll keep trying until you get it right. That's confidence. You will work without setting limits on what you think you can do. You'll cast a wide net for dreams and figure out how to make them reality. You'll work hard. You won't whine. You'll ask when you need help. You'll take inspiration from the legions of women who came before you, the ones who define what it means to be So Boss.

WE ARE WOMEN, HEAR US ROAR

We use a lot of terms to refer to ourselves—*girls, women, chicks, bosses*—and we mean no disrespect to those who fought hard-won battles in the name of women's rights. We know we could be calling ourselves "womyn" or ditching references to our gender altogether, and we aren't promoting a return to backward thinking. We aren't belittling ourselves by using the word *girl*. On the contrary, we're taking the word back. Historically, some people have used "girl" as an insult or as a way of conveying a juvenile, less capable image, because they think women can't do everything just as well as men can. But we know they're wrong, and we know that being a girl is something to be proud of. As women, we've had to fight for our rights and for respect, and that fight just adds to our strength.

WE ALL EXPRESS DIFFERENT ASPECTS OF OUR SELF-IMAGES AT DIFFERENT TIMES. We are all girls, women, chicks, dames, broads, and goddesses. We all work hard, and we deserve to call ourselves whatever we want. A girl who runs a business is no less powerful than a woman who runs a business. We are all harnessing our inner Eleanor Roosevelts and working to create entrepreneurial projects. That's what being So Boss means. And that's what it means to be a girl, a woman, or whatever you want to call yourself.

SO LET'S NOT HAVE ANY CONFUSION ABOUT WHO WE MEAN WHEN WE'RE DESCRIBING BOSSES: WE'RE DESCRIBING OURSELVES. We're describing girls who want to start businesses and those who are already running the show. We're describing ladies with attitude who won't take no for an answer—not where their dreams are concerned. We're describing J.K. Rowling, Janelle Monae, Amelia Earheart, Mo'ne Davis, Gloria Steinem, Oprah Winfrey, Lucille Ball, Linda Sarsour, Chelsea Clinton, Taylor Swift, Malala Yousafzai, Sofia Vergara, Aung San Suu Kyi, Michelle Obama, Tavi Gevinson, Samantha Bee. And we're describing you.

JUST ONE MORE THING

There will be a lot of "just one more things" in this book—many concepts require a little afterthought or footnote for clarity or nuance, so be sure to take note. Sometimes you might find the "just one more things" to be even more valuable than the things themselves.

IN THIS CASE, THE FOOTNOTE IS ABOUT BEING GOOD TO YOUR FELLOW BOSSES. Never cut another female down. We're all here working hard to create something new, to motivate change in the world, to start something that matters. Some people may succeed seemingly easily, or it looks like they got a leg up. You may think someone's idea is ridiculous and you can't imagine how it succeeded. Or you may see someone succeeding who you know isn't a very nice person.

HOLD YOUR TONGUE. We don't get ahead by disparaging one another. The expression "a rising tide floats all boats" applies to us—especially since women need to work together and support one another in a world where we haven't always been taken seriously. Where one woman succeeded there is room for another. One person's rise paves the way for the next one to follow, and we don't need to boost ourselves by stepping on others. Be nice to everyone. Be fair. Treat other people the way you'd like to be treated. You never know who you may come in contact with later. Root for one another.

"WE CANNOT SUCCEED WHEN HALF OF US ARE HELD BACK. WE CALL UPON OUR SISTERS AROUND THE WORLD TO BE BRAVE, TO EMBRACE THE STRENGTH WITHIN THEMSELVES AND REALIZE THEIR FULL POTENTIAL."

—Malala Yousafzai, winner of the Nobel Peace Prize

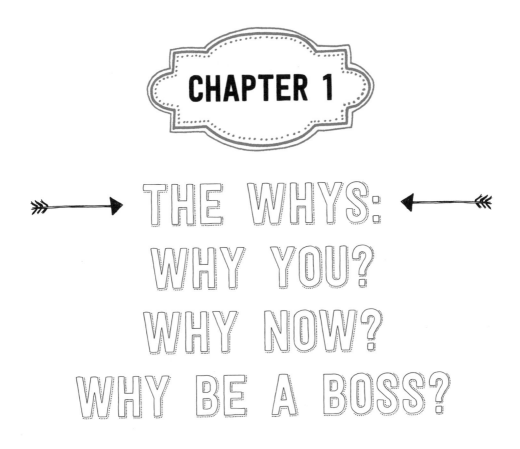

CHAPTER 1

THE WHYS: WHY YOU? WHY NOW? WHY BE A BOSS?

People sometimes talk about wishing they could go back and do things all over again with the benefit of knowledge that only comes with experience. As we go along in life and in the business world, we learn lessons we wish we'd known when we were younger.

But the other reason people talk about wanting to go back is that they realize there's a freedom in *not* knowing everything. When you haven't had mountains of experience, you don't have as many voices inside your head questioning your every move. You haven't been told no a hundred times, and for all you know, you'll never hear a discouraging word. There's a beautiful luxury in making plans without feeling constraints. So for now, make use of the fact that you don't know everything, including your limitations. It's Part Two of thinking big. Think without self-censorship.

The advantages of youth: an attitude of invincibility, a little stupidity, fresh ideas, ideas that come from a "do what you know, do what you love" mentality, tech savvy.

What young entrepreneurs still need to learn: the money stuff, the management stuff, the grown-up stuff that isn't fun but is necessary for success beyond the walls of your bedroom.

THE WALLS ARE COMING DOWN

Twenty or even ten years ago, if someone had floated the idea of 16- and 17-year-olds running business with profit margins and employees, there would've been a lot of disbelief. Maybe even snide laughter. No more. Today there are young entrepreneurs outearning their elders and starting businesses at a faster rate than ever before. They have ideas. They have energy. They are ready to get started. It's time for you to join them.

BOSSES CAN BE 5. THEY CAN BE 17. THEY CAN BE 20. People may still be skeptical, especially if they are older and haven't had a lot of exposure to young entrepreneurs with big ideas. Don't let them discourage you. Think of every naysayer as an opportunity to educate a new person about what young women can do. This doesn't mean you'll encounter resistance wherever you go. But if and when you do, step over it and keep going.

There are amazing opportunities today for entrepreneurs of any age, especially now that technology makes everything faster, easier, and more accessible. You can do business with someone who lives halfway across the country—or the world—without ever having a face-to-face meeting (although face-to-face meetings are useful). You can use technology to set up your own website, launch your own Twitter feed, create your own brand, and market yourself. It doesn't matter how old you are. If you have a great idea and you work at getting the word out, you can find an audience or a market.

TEN FABULOUS GIRL BOSSES YOU SHOULD GET TO KNOW

1.
MADAME C. J. WALKER, aka Sarah Breedlove, who started a business of hair care products for black women and became the first black female millionaire.

2.
OPRAH WINFREY, who got her first talk show at 21 and has been blazing a trail for women who are So Boss ever since.

3.
NELLIE BLY, aka Elizabeth Cochran, who was 20 years old when she wrote a story for a Pittsburgh newspaper about injustices suffered by divorced women, a taboo subject at the time. But people read her stories, and she was hired as the newspaper's first female reporter.

6.
SARA BLAKELY, founder of Spanx, a $150 million business selling slimming undergarments with no visible panty lines.

4.
JANE McGONIGAL, world-renowned alternate-reality game designer and founder of SuperBetter, an online game that has helped nearly half a million people battle neurological disorders and traumatic brain injuries.

5.
LIMOR FRIED, computer engineer and sole owner and founder of Adafruit, an open-source hardware company that offers online education in building electronics as well as selling over $40 million in electronic product kits annually.

9.
MARIE CURIE, who at age 24 railed against the doors closed to women interested in science and went on to win two Nobel Prizes for her work on radioactivity, one in physics and one in chemistry.

7.
LUCILLE BALL, America's original comedian-producer–empire builder, an earlier generation's Julia Louis-Dreyfus or Lena Dunham. Queen of physical comedy, she was also often the hardest-working person on the set, learning to run her own production company and winning four Emmy awards in the process.

8.
CATERINA FAKE, cofounder of the photo management site Flickr (now owned by Yahoo), founder of the travel hub Findery, and former chairwoman of the board at Etsy.

10.
SHARON VOSMEK, CEO of Astia, a San Francisco–based nonprofit that helps find investors for high-growth startups led by women.

ANANTOMY OF A GIRL BOSS

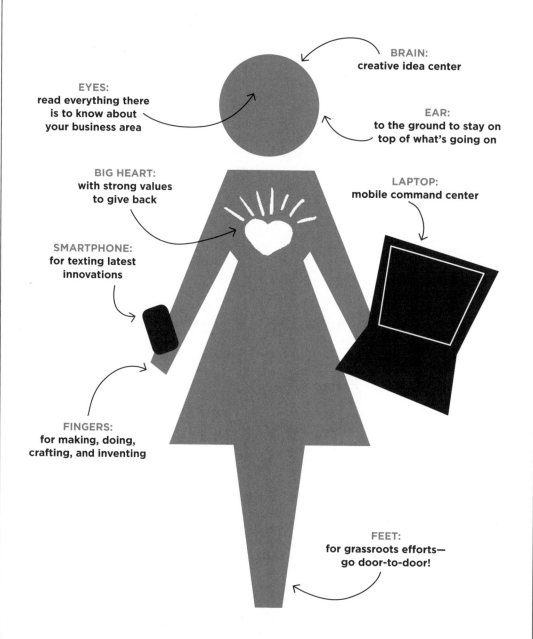

BRAIN:
creative idea center

EYES:
read everything there
is to know about
your business area

EAR:
to the ground to stay on
top of what's going on

BIG HEART:
with strong values
to give back

LAPTOP:
mobile command center

SMARTPHONE:
for texting latest
innovations

FINGERS:
for making, doing,
crafting, and inventing

FEET:
for grassroots efforts—
go door-to-door!

YOU ARE SO BOSS

OF COURSE YOU ARE. If running your own business is something you want to do, you are Boss. Even before you hatch your first business idea or jot down the bare bones of a business plan, you are Boss. Being Boss means you're a little bit badass, a little bit bossy, a little bit stubborn, a little bit spirited, and a little—well, actually, a lot—persistent.

GETTING HELP DOESN'T TAKE AWAY YOUR BOSS-NESS. You will need advice from people around you. You may need to borrow money. You will have mentors and role models. Being a smart boss means getting help when you need it instead of reinventing the wheel.

A BOSS ISN'T A DIVA. If you're shy, if you don't always feel like speaking in public, if you don't think of yourself as a leader, if you worry no one else sees you the way you see yourself, if you are scared, if you are intimidated, if you are uncertain, can you still be Boss material? *Yes!*

YOU HAVE POWER

You may not realize it, but people who run companies and sell products—especially ones aimed at teenage girls—want you. They're interested in what you think. They want to know what you like. **YOU ARE PART OF A VERY SOUGHT-AFTER, INFLUENTIAL GROUP OF CONSUMERS.** Often these companies are run by older executives, frequently men, usually relying on research. They're trying to figure out how to get your attention.

And here's where you have a distinct advantage over them: They are not you. They want to know what you like and what you want to buy, but they have to take surveys and ask questions to find out. You don't have to do that—you already know what you like. You know what your friends wear and read and would buy if only it existed. Make it exist. Start your business using firsthand research. **USE THAT POWER.**

YOU BUILD COMMUNITIES

You don't go a day without connecting with your friends, letting them know what you're doing and how you're doing it. You read each other's stories on Snapchat, you "like" each other's photos on Facebook, you LOL via text, and you tweet what you're thinking. That's in addition to hanging out with your friends, talking about what you like and how you plan to change the world. That connectedness will work well for you when you launch and grow your business. **THAT SAME COMMUNITY OF FRIENDS AND FAMILY WILL BE YOUR FIRST TEST MARKET OF CUSTOMERS.** They'll tell a friend, and their friends will tell more friends. Your community is an important driving force for your business, but the best part is that you built your community just for the sake of being surrounded by and connected to people you love. Your relationships are genuine. You help your friends and they help you. And that community will build things—together.

MEET OUR BOSSES

FORTUNATELY, YOU DO NOT HAVE TO REINVENT THE WHEEL. You can learn from the talented, experienced Boss girls who took up the reins before you and are here to share their stories and hard-earned lessons from the trenches. You can follow the ups, downs, challenges, and thrills of starting and running a business by reading about bosses like you, who started with an idea and grew it into a full-fledged enterprise. These awesome girl Bosses are putting the lessons we'll teach you here into action. Check out how they do things while you progress and grow your own business.

THE BOSSES IN THIS BOOK WILL INSPIRE YOU. They'll share how they handled the same kinds of challenges you will face. That means two things: you are not alone— many Bosses have faced the same hurdles you may find in front of you—and you don't have to find your way without information and advice.

SO, GET INSPIRED. Meet our Bosses.

NIHARIKA BEDEKAR didn't expect to have a life-changing event at age 7. But when she got her first period at that young age—compared with an average age of 13, according to national statistics at the time—her eyes were opened not just to how it felt to be different from her peers, but to how she could offer support to other girls. She realized how debilitating body image issues could be to a girl's developing self-esteem, and she learned that many future disorders have their root in events that take place during puberty. So she started Power Up, a nonprofit organization dedicated to helping girls understand what their bodies will go through at puberty, so it's not scary or taboo. When not studying at Stanford University, she was working as a software engineering intern on the Apple Watch team. Niharika talks to groups of young girls about age-appropriate behavior, confronting unrealistic media images, and being comfortable with themselves. Follow her at twitter.com/niharikabedekar.

CHENTAL-SONG BEMBRY loved reading and watching TV when she was growing up in Somerset, New Jersey, but it bothered her that she didn't see characters who looked like her. So at the age of 10, she created a book series called The Honey Bunch Kids, which evolved into a series of stories based on middle schoolers who meet one day when they miss the bus and have to walk to school in the rain. The books teach lessons about compassion, bullying, and friendship. By the time she was a senior at Hampton University in Virginia, Chental-Song had sold more than 3,000 copies of her books and was working on a graphic novel and an animated TV show based on her characters. Connect with her at twitter.com/chentalsong.

DEEPIKA BODAPATI has put blood, sweat, and tears into her passion for science. Especially blood. She spent her junior high and high school years devising science fair projects with real-world applications, like creating a test strip to detect whether vegetables were contaminated with bacteria like E. coli or salmonella. That led to partnering with a friend, Tanay Tandon, and creating a company, Athelas (it just happens to be a healing herb in *Lord of the Rings*), which has developed a portable device to screen a drop of blood for a whole host of diseases. Yes, she used her own blood for testing at first. Using computer vision and algorithms, the Athelas device can produce results on a smartphone in minutes and at a fraction of the cost of other testing devices. While in college at the University of Southern California, Deepika won first place and $25,000 in seed money in the 2015 Silicon Beach @ USC competition for new ventures in emerging technology and enrolled in the Y Combinator summer program, in which a clinical trial proved 100% effective. The company is currently expanding in Mexico and India. Check it out at **athelas.com**.

JULIETTE BRINDAK BLAKE was just 13 years old when she founded Miss O and Friends, a safe social media site for tween girls, based on characters she created and drew when she was 11. She has since grown Miss O and Friends into a multimillion-dollar business that gives tween girls a place to socialize, play games, get advice, and build self-esteem. The site has more than 1 million monthly unique visitors. Juliette's company is now greenlighted for a scripted series with the largest video platform in the world, loosely based on Miss O and Friends, who are middle schoolers working on a website and the day-to-day drama in their lives. Running the business while still in high school was a juggling act of studying for tests while meeting with investors and growing a company. Now out of college, Juliette runs the business full-time. Check out Miss O at **missoandfriends.com**.

ALEXANDRA (ALEX) DOUWES and NELLIE MORRIS created a company that exemplifies the adage "do what you know" (and figure out what you don't know along the way). At age 23 they founded Purpose Generation, a consulting firm that helps iconic brands better understand and engage millennials. They are experts in that coveted target market, being part of it themselves, and work with a team of young strategists and freelancers to help companies connect with the next generation of consumers and talent. Their clients include Campbell's Soup, Wells Fargo Bank, and AARP. After graduating from Princeton University, Nellie helped launch the first regulated social stock market in South Africa and was chosen to be one of 100 innovators to fly from San Francisco to London as part of British Airways "UnGrounded: Innovation Lab in the Sky." Alex grew up in London and the Netherlands before moving to the United States to study international relations and play field hockey at Princeton. She started her career with a short stint at the Acumen Fund before joining a global management consulting practice. The two friends and business partners met in college but found out years later that they were born in the same London hospital. Some things are just meant to be. Check them out at **purposegeneration.com**.

DEBBIE FUNG was 23 when she cofounded Yoga Tree, a yoga studio in Toronto, Canada. Now, she co-owns yoga studios and has plans to open more. She and her partner, Jason (they met at university and later married), traveled to India after college. There they learned about yoga and Ayurvedic medicine, and when they got back, they were certain that working for other people's companies was not for them. So they took the money they had planned to spend buying a condo and used it to start Yoga Tree, which now offers some 2,000 classes per month. It was recognized as one of Canada's fastest-growing companies, and they made yoga, which was still obscure when they were getting started, a mainstream fitness necessity. Get out your yoga mat and check out Yoga Tree at **yogatree.ca**.

FE MAIDENS (pronounced "Iron Maidens"—Fe is the chemical symbol for iron) is an all-girl robotics team at Bronx High School of Science, a magnet school in New York City. Their goal is to further the role of women in the fields of science and engineering and to encourage more girls to participate in these fields. The team of 60 works to foster a greater love and appreciation for science and technology and to promote the ideals of FIRST (For Recognition of Science and Technology) and to give their members the opportunity to advance their skills and knowledge. Through competitions and teamwork, they aim to dissolve the prejudices against women in technology and engineering. Team captain Charlotte collected the team's advice for this book. Check them out at **femaidens.wordpress.com**.

From the time **ALYSON GREENFIELD** went to see a play at age 6, she knew she wanted to be on stage. Even though no one in her family played music, she begged her parents for piano lessons until they agreed, which allowed her to begin her singer/songwriter career at age 10. She plays drums, keyboards, and guitar, as well as the chord organ and synthesizer. Inspired by the all-female festival Lilith Fair, she started her own indie women's music festival, which grew to five stages on three nights in New York City. Tinderbox Music Festival ran for four years straight and showcased more than 100 emerging female musicians from all over the world. Alyson now plays music at venues around New York City, writes musical scores for films, and produces events focused on social justice and arts empowerment in the classroom. She also teaches English at Hunter College. Find her at **alysongreenfield.com**.

PRISCILLA GUO attended Hunter College High School in New York City. There, she was president of Girl Up, UNICEF, and Science Club. She was also a poetry ambassador for Girls Write Now as well as one of Business Insider's "Most Impressive High School Graduates" in 2014. In Priscilla's junior year, then-Mayor Bloomberg appointed her to serve on the New York City Youth Board, where she advised on the growth and development of youth programming. Priscilla also founded a summer youth program to teach computer coding to public housing students in Harlem, where she teaches every summer, exposing kids to potential careers and pathways to success. Priscilla won a prestigious scholarship to the US Senate Youth Program for students interested in public service and was one of two to represent New York City in the nation's capital. As part of the program, she met with then-President Barack Obama, Justice Antonin Scalia, and International Monetary Fund director Christine Lagarde. Priscilla studies technology, policy, and society at Harvard University, where she serves as copresident of Harvard Women in Computer Science and copresident of Harvard Undergraduate Women in Business. At the Harvard Institute of Politics, she is the technology director and STEAM (science, technology, engineering, art, and mathematics) chair. Priscilla writes for the *Harvard Political Review* and and is interested in exploring the intersection between politics and technology. Find her at twitter.com/**priscillawguo**.

GABRIELLE JORDAN started Jewelz of Jordan, selling gem-studded necklaces, earrings, and bracelets, when she was 9 years old. Once she learned how to make jewelry on YouTube, there was no stopping her. At 16 years old, she expanded her collection to include her Girlz line of jewelry, each piece of which comes with an inspirational message for young girls, and the Tigerlily collection, a portion of whose proceeds go toward the Tigerlily Foundation to provide services to girls and women diagnosed with breast cancer. Gabrielle, who lives in Bowie, Maryland, is the author of the book *The Making of a Young Entrepreneur* and runs the ExCEL Youth Mentoring Institute, which helps young entrepreneurs launch their businesses. Find her at **gabriellejordaninspires.com**.

NEEKA MASHOUF credits her dad with her love of engineering and entrepreneurship. When she was a kid, he gave her electrical components and circuit boards and let her create . . . fruit with electronic components sticking out? No matter, the lessons stayed with her. At UC Berkeley, Neeka pursued simultaneous degrees in materials engineering and business administration and leads the battery unit of CalSol, UC Berkeley's solar vehicle team. She was a builder of the solar car and drove the car in the American Solar Challenge, a 2,000-mile (3,200 km) road race across the United States that started with a lap race around a Formula One racetrack in Pittsburgh and then took to the road from Ohio to South Dakota, driving through national parks to celebrate the National Park Service's centennial. She also founded a startup at UC Berkeley's Social Innovator OnRamp incubator aimed at providing renewable energy to people around the world who don't have access to electricity. Before this she designed and built an inflatable solar oven and a solar cell phone charger. At age 13, along with her twin sister, she started a company to sell their handmade crystal jewelry and reached international sales. Check her out at **neekamashouf.com**.

Originally from Israel, **NAAMA RAZ-YASEEF** knew she wanted to work in the field of ecology and environmental science but after working at a private environmental consulting company, she felt her work wasn't having enough impact. So she moved halfway across the world to study in Northern California and work at the Lawrence Berkeley National Laboratory. She learned that in rural Zimbabwe, where it rains only a couple of months out of the year, women struggled to grow staple foods in the drier seasons, and they had to carry water from a river in buckets balanced on their heads, up a steep hill, just to get water to their crops. So she founded a nonprofit pilot program to create a watering method for the community and developed an affordable mobile irrigation system to water crops year-round. Find out more about what Naama is up to at http://rynaama. wixsite.com/naama-razyaseef/home.

CHELSEA SILER is a golfer, ultramarathoner, and senior communications officer for the Canadian Broadcasting Company/Radio-Canada (where she connected the network's brand with Canadians using social media during the Rio Olympics), as well as founder and owner of the public relations and marketing firm Five & Vine in Vancouver, BC. She's in charge of communication, brand management, and crisis management in the digital and social space for Canada's second most recognizable brand. But let's back up a minute: yes, we said ultramarathoner. That means she runs 100-mile (160 km) races and doesn't have any intention of slowing down. Chelsea works hard and if she wants to take on a new job responsibility that seems beyond her pay grade, she just asks and makes it clear she's there to do the job—even an unglamorous job if it's a means to an end—until she reaches her goal. It's that ultramarathon mentality. Find her at twitter.com/chelseasiler.

"DON'T BE INTIMIDATED BY WHAT YOU DON'T KNOW. THAT CAN BE YOUR GREATEST STRENGTH AND ENSURE THAT YOU DO THINGS DIFFERENTLY FROM EVERYONE ELSE."

—Sara Blakely, founder of Spanx

CHAPTER 2

IT ALL STARTS WITH
AN IDEA

Anything can be a business. We'll say it again. *Anything* can be a business. Your angry rants at bad drivers? A stand-up comedy routine or song lyric material. Your aunt's donated closet of vintage clothes that aren't your style? An online vintage store. Your style that everyone on campus wants to copy? A personal shopper or stylist. Your science projects in the basement? An emerging biotech company.

So don't get hung up thinking that the things you love to do most in the world don't seem very businessworthy. They might be not at first—but that doesn't mean you can't get them there. Cast a wide net for yourself and really think. (Take a walk around the neighborhood. Getting your feet moving has an incredible way of getting your mind moving too.)

WHAT HAVE YOU ALWAYS LIKED TO DO? Don't self-censor. Don't tell yourself, *Yeah, but that's not really a business*. Make a list, and don't feel embarrassed if it includes things like hanging out with your friends, painting your nails, googling weird science facts, and studying for engineering tests. We can create businesses out of all those things. That's the fun part.

Alex Douwes and Nellie Morris came up with the idea for their business, Purpose Generation, because of common attitudes and opinions they observed in their peers.

◇◇

ALEX AND NELLIE

It all started over coffee back in 2012 when we were discussing why so many of our peers were unhappy in their jobs. A lot of them were leaving the corporate world for startups in the hopes of finding a greater sense of purpose and agency, looking to have an impact. We recognized that large corporations have significant resources but often don't understand how to leverage these to retain top young talent and engage millennial consumers. We discovered that boardrooms are filled with 50-year-old-plus men talking about what their kids want and realized that, as millennials, we were uniquely able to advise them on how to remain relevant.

Instead of making assumptions about what our generation wants— or assuming that our own opinion reflects that of everyone else—we decided to build a tribe of 18- to 35-year-olds to act as our in-house insights engine. Our tribe is made up of engaged, passionate consumers who want to co-create new products and services alongside brands. We kick off every project by tapping into our tribe and continue to come back for them for feedback and gut checks along the way to ensure that the consumer voice is an integral part of every solution. Instead of sitting down with research participants in a sterile environment like traditional market research firms do, however, we connect with them as peers and make the process as engaging and fun as possible. Then we translate these insights into a language our clients can understand. This has been a huge differentiator for us.

FIND YOUR THING

They key to any good business is coming up with something you can provide that other people want. Sounds simple, and it can be. Sure, there will be hitches along the way, but if this wasn't challenging, it wouldn't be worth doing.

YOU KNOW WHAT YOU LIKE TO DO. It's that thing you always have to put aside so you can get to your homework. Then, as soon as you get the chance, you're back looking at videos on coding and trying to hack into your parents' laptops. Or writing your blog. Or makng smoothies. So take those interests and think about how to pursue them big-time. That should be the starting point of your business: the thing you love to do so much that you'll sneak time away from everything else to do it. If you love it, you'll keep at it until you're good at it. And if you're good at it, you'll want to spend more time on it. Once you've mastered it, you can build it into a successful venture.

HERE IS WHERE YOU GET TO STRETCH YOUR IMAGINATION and think far and wide about how what you like to do could be a business. Don't limit yourself to enterprises that sound like traditional businesses. If you and your friends always start each hang session by pulling out a bag of clothes and swapping them, realize that maybe there's a new business in clothing swap parties. Throw in a small entry fee and some food and your idea turns into a fun, profitable night. Art, politics, nonprofit work, writing: any of those can be your launching pad. The only thing that qualifies a new venture as the right venture is that it's something you enjoy. Let's start there and take the next few chapters to figure out how to turn that thing you like into something you pursue avidly. That something is your business and you are the Boss.

For Neeka Mashouf, that thing was a solar car.

NEEKA

I've always been passionate about renewable energy, especially solar energy. Ever since I first learned about it, I have been in love with solar energy. . . . If cars were powered by the sun, there would be so much power for change. This project is student-built, student-run. People on the team had an idea of what they thought was cool, that they thought would have an impact, and they just ran with it. The things we do are things no one has done before, exploring this unknown frontier.

I'm super passionate about this. The car team has been around since 1990 and has built generations of vehicles. We just finished our eighth-generation car. It's gone from three wheels and superheavy to now incredibly light, with the same mileage as a Tesla—250 miles (400 km) on single charge on battery pack. If you drive at 45 miles (72 km) per hour, you can drive indefinitely on sun power. The energy in equals the energy out.

People have described the car as looking like a spaceship or boat. It's really aerodynamic and thin from the side. Sleek. It's beautiful, with a cockpit for the driver. This car and past cars seat one. The next car that we're designing is going to be a multiseater solar-powered sportscar. We're getting closer to the vision of having a solar car in society.

START BY MAKING A LIST

GO ON, GET OUT A PIECE OF PAPER. NUMBER IT FROM 1 TO 20. Start listing things you like to do, or even things you've always wanted to do but haven't had the chance to do. List them with abandon. Don't censor yourself or tell yourself they're not business-worthy. We'll get to the how-tos later. What are things you would do on a day when you had no other plans? Your list can include things like coding, going hiking, throwing a ball with your dog. Maybe you enjoy reading magazine advice columns or long-distance running? Whatever you like, write it down.

THEN MAKE A NEW LIST. Write down 5 things that really scare you. Do you hate speaking to strangers? Dislike talking about yourself? Hate being indoors? These things are good to know, too. Things that scare you are not reasons to choose or not choose a type of new venture. They're things to know about yourself at the outset. Knowing them will help you deal with them and overcome them.

NOW HAVE A LOOK AT YOUR FIRST LIST. There are the activities that you simply love, the things you'd do for free, things you'd rather be doing than almost anything else. There's also likely another category among the items on your list: things you're good at. Being good at something can be reason enough to like it. But by acknowledging your skill, you're distinguishing things you merely find fun from things you can do better than others. That's where you can begin to find the seeds of the business you will start and run.

EVERY BUSINESS STARTS WITH AN IDEA. It doesn't have to be a never-before-thought-of idea, but it has to be an original take on an idea.

Here's how Chental-Song Bembry came up with The Honey Bunch Kids.

◇◇

CHENTAL-SONG

The inspiration started when I was 10 years old. I loved reading and writing and loved to watch cartoons. But I didn't see any main characters on TV who looked like me. My characters Dizzy, Cheeks, and Stuart are all in sixth grade, 11 years old. They're based on parts of myself, my friends, my family, and kids I knew at school. All three characters were starting sixth grade and didn't know one another, but they met at the same bus stop. I wrote about kids in middle school learning to get along, exploring such themes as respect, empathy, why not to bully, and peer pressure.

Right now I'm working on turning the books into an animated series and brand. What Dora the Explorer and SpongeBob have, I want for the Honey Bunch Kids. I'm working on a comic book deal and finding a production company to partner with. We have a theme song, animation—and cool dance moves.

IDENTIFY A NEED

It almost sounds so obvious that we sometimes forget: the best ideas come from some-one looking around and thinking, *Why isn't there a ___ for that?* If you're wondering why a solution to a clear problem doesn't exist, chances are others are thinking the same thing. Ask yourself, What are all the big or small problems I can think of that no one has solved yet? You may have some really big problems on your list, like coming up with alternative fuel solutions and restoring the water table in drought-ravaged areas. Or you could tackle a smaller problem: Why aren't tights more durable?

Some challenges stem from your hopes for the world around us: less pollution, more trees in urban areas, more equitable access to organic food. Others are a matter of thinking outside the design box.

When Naama Raz-Yaseef started her nonprofit in Zimbabwe, she was trying to solve a very concrete problem in a single village: how to design a pump that would move water from a river up a steep slope and into gardens where crops were growing. The community needed an irrigation system, but they lacked the resources for the necessary power source.

NAAMA

My solution was very simple: to bring in irrigation pumps that were really small and cheap. They're like the sump pumps many Americans have at their houses. But because there was no electricity in this village we decided to install mobile solar panels that cost less than $100 each. The pump suctions water from the river and pushes it up through a hose to a container at the top of the hill, from which a drip irrigation system runs the water through the gardens. It's a simple, well-known working solution.

I believe in small scale, working with a specific community and under-standing their needs. We test the system with the women and train them so they'll become experts. They can train others, thus creating a source of income for the community.

>>> → QUICK! ← <<<

LIST 10 JOBS

YOU WISH EXISTED.

MAYBE NOW THEY WILL!

1. _____

2. _____

3. _____

4. _____

5. _____

6. _____

7. _____

8. _____

9. _____

10. _____

JUST ONE MORE THING

WE HEAR IT A LOT: DO WHAT YOU LOVE! And while that is great advice—who wouldn't want to have a job they love?—it's not the whole picture. The reality is that work is work, and even doing what you love comes with a lot of things you might not love so much. You may even hate them. That's fine—just make sure you can handle having them in your life. For example, if writing takes you to a blissful place of creative freedom, you may want to find a way to make it your business. And you should. Write a novel, start a blog, create a magazine, make a movie. But realize that there are other elements involved: selling your work, marketing yourself, negotiating, dealing with other people, being told no, rewriting according to other people's ideas that don't necessarily match your own. **NO ONE LOVES EVERYTHING ALL THE TIME.** There are bound to be bumps and scratches in the process of launching anything you decide to do. So make a commitment to yourself that you will persevere in spite of the things you may not love. They're part of the package.

As the Bronx High School of Science Fe (Iron) Maidens learned, perseverance pays off.

◇◇

CHARLOTTE, TEAM CAPTAIN

Being on a robotics team is a lot of work. We met twice a week year-round and every day but Sunday for six weeks during build season. We spent time at home planning out our meetings and gave up our weekends and summers for video calls discussing design and strategy. But in the end it was definitely worth it. As frustrating as robotics can sometimes be, when nothing works and deadlines are approaching, by the end of those six weeks, when you have a (hopefully) fully functioning robot competing with teams from across the world, you know that all the time and energy you spent in the end paid off. Even though you may have had to stay up way too late way too often or missed out on hanging out with some of your friends, you still got to spend time with your friends on the team, doing what you love to do.

QUICK!
LIST 10 PROBLEMS
IN NEED OF SOLUTIONS.

1. _____

2. _____

3. _____

4. _____

5. _____

6. _____

7. _____

8. _____

9. _____

10. _____

"NO ONE CHANGES THE WORLD
WHO ISN'T OBSESSED."

—Billie Jean King, former World No. 1 professional tennis player

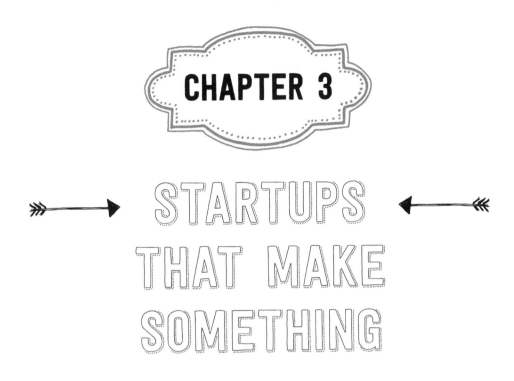

CHAPTER 3

STARTUPS THAT MAKE SOMETHING

One of the very basic segments of our economy is called "goods and services." Those are all things people need and pay for—they make the economy hum along prosperously. But what are goods and services?

GOODS ARE THINGS. They are made by a person or a machine; you can use them and hold them in your hands. Earrings, cherry pies, hydroponic gardens, computer paper, T-shirts, blood scanners, solar cars—they're all goods. And for them to be available for purchase, someone has to make them. That requires hard materials and a method for manufacturing. It doesn't have to mean you go into business with a factory. You can be your own factory when you're starting out. But you need supplies and a place to put everything together, so your business will have a different set of startup needs than a business that provides a service.

If you're building furniture from recycled barn doors or screen-printing your designs on trucker hats, you're producing goods. Dentist appointments and art classes are services. If you're advising clients on social media strategies or composing theme music or writing algorithms to solve problems, you're running a service business. We'll talk more about services in a bit—but first let's go deeper into businesses that sell goods. To begin with, you need something to show the world. You need them to see what you can do.

MAKING A PROTOTYPE

The word *prototype* might conjure up an image of a complicated lab, but it's really just something to show other people what your product looks like and what it can do. It means you're making a few samples of your work.

Whether your product is a rainproof poncho, a software program that stores passwords, or a special juice blend, you will need to make at least one prime example to show. Start by experimenting. Use whatever resources you have at school or at an extracurricular class to fill in for tools you may not have handy at home. Maybe you've come up with a wearable microscope and you can use the after-school lab to design and build it. Rally whatever resources you have available to help you build out your first working sample device.

Don't worry if your design doesn't quite turn out the way you planned when it comes to life. All products are going to involve systematic tinkering and refining.

Here's how Gabrielle Jordan came to start Jewelz of Jordan when she was 9 years old, and how she makes her prototypes today.

GABRIELLE

When I was really young, I started being attracted to jewelry. I would go to my mom's jewelry counter and look at the pieces and want to wear them around the house. But the difference between me and another girl who loves jewelry was when I saw a broken earring on my mom's counter or on the sidewalk I'd immediately have an idea of what I could do with it. When I was seven, I heard about YouTube, so I would go on YouTube every day and watch jewelry videos, look at different designs, and teach myself. I was always drawn to very upscale, elegant, classic vintage styles. I love that look and that's what I went for.

When I'm creating a piece, it starts off with figuring out the design. How do we want it to look and how will it appeal to our market? I'm not a great sketch artist, but I'm able to represent what I'm trying to design, and I use pens and paper and a digital platform because it's easier to understand. I work out how I want it to represent the line for the season.

Then I go to gem and jewelry shows. People have booths with large varieties of stones, clasps, spacers. I use high-quality crystals and pearls, semiprecious and precious stones. We figure out colors we want to work with, find the beads that work best with the design. This part is fun—being able to have a creation come to life, to see what we're going to create. Then we come back to studio and start laying out how we want things to look. Sometimes the drawing doesn't look as good as we expected, so we do a lot of deleting and trying again, going back and forth. I really enjoy the process because creativity is a huge part of me.

DON'T FORGET THAT PART: ENJOY THE PROCESS. None of this should feel like the worst homework assignment you can imagine. If it does, shift gears. If you are feeling out of ideas or creatively stuck, step back and do something else you enjoy—go for a run, cook up something delicious, grab your pals for a movie night—and then when you are feeling refreshed, try again. Try and try it again. Maybe you're crafting a new iPhone case out of specialized rubber that also works to erase pencil marks or take handprints off walls. Start mixing your rubber recipe and try out a few different weights, sizes, and shapes until you come up with the best version to show other people.

IF YOU'RE MAKING SOMETHING INVOLVING FOOD, for example, prototyping is when you work out the recipes. Making organic granola? Try all the different combinations until you have several really good ones. Test them on everyone you know. Get your recipes down. Figure out your packaging. When you get the chance to present someone with your product for the first time, make a good impression. Bring your cookies to a party and serve them for dessert. Pay attention to how people react. Who is eating them? Just the kids? Are they peeling off the chocolate chips and eating those first or are they going for the gooey middles? This is the kind of research companies pay big bucks for, so don't miss an opportunity to get information for free.

GO FOR VARIETY

WHEN YOU FIRST BEGIN SELLING YOUR IDEA, SHOW IT WELL. Take the time beforehand to create lots of different prototypes. Some people are challenged when it comes to imagining possibilities. Instead of simply talking about what a wearable microscope can do, bring a demonstration to potential clients. Instead of bringing one small plaid dog bed and telling a shop owner that you can also make large ones in corduroy, or other ones with pockets, and still others with attached cat toys for felines, bring examples of everything you can make. Don't give anyone the opportunity to imagine the wrong thing or suppose you can't really pull something off when you know you can.

If you're screen-printing sweatshirts, show designs on the front, the back, the sleeves. Show designs for kids, women, and men. Personalize a few. Offer options. If you're baking cupcakes, bring a variety of flavors, only put the best-looking ones in a box, and decorate everything.

Don't get ahead of yourself, worrying about capital budgets or vertical integration yet—yes, those are real—**JUST START MAKING YOUR PRODUCT.** Sew a skirt, write a graphic novel, build a working model, write a concerto, construct a mousetrap car. Work out the miscalculations and refine your concept. At the beginning of your business venture, focus on its potential.

NUTS AND BOLTS, LITERALLY

YOU'LL NEED SUPPLIES. You may need to hit the hardware store. Or the art supply store. Or the lumberyard. Figure out where to get what you need at the best price. Start comparing prices online and in stores. Don't forget to factor in shipping costs to get those seemingly inexpensive online supplies to your doorstep. It does you no good to find a $1.99 glue gun with 50 cartridges when it will cost $13.99 to ship it. Better to pick up one for $5.99 at a local art supply store.

This may not matter for the first sample product you're making, but once you have orders for a dozen or a thousand, **YOU'LL NEED TO KNOW WHERE TO GET YOUR SUPPLIES IN BULK.** To make smart spending decisions, you'll need to have an accurate cost for what it takes to make not just one fabulous item but many. Don't forget to factor in intangible costs, like the time it takes to make each one, or overhead expenses like rental costs for machinery or workspace.

THAT THING YOU CREATE MIGHT BE ART

NOT EVERYTHING IS ALWAYS CLEAR CUT. You know that if you're making scarves out of recycled cashmere sweater pieces that you're making a product that you can hold in your hand. It's a tangible thing.

What if the thing you're doing is a performance? Is it only a startup if you're starting a theater company or a theater festival, or is it also a startup if you're launching your acting career? We think you know the answer already, but just to be clear, when you're creating an artistic product, whether it is on the page or in performance, it counts. Of course it's a startup. You are launching yourself and your talent, your expression of something you want to share, into the world and letting people know they can hire you or pay you to sing for them or perform magic tricks at a gallery opening.

MIXING ART WITH BUSINESS

WHEN YOU'RE CREATIVE AND TALENTED, there's almost nothing better than pursuing your art full-time. Whether you're a painter or a musician or a playwright, you are Boss, and you're your own Boss. There are specific challenges that go along with turning something creative—which may also be your passion—into a job. You will be criticized sometimes, and it will feel personal. You will struggle sometimes, and that will make you question whether you're as talented as someone else.

YOU WILL ALSO NEED TO HAVE A BUSINESS MENTALITY about something that is, at its heart, art. It can get tricky. When you want to get paid to write your blog, you will have to be mindful of what advertisers (likely your source of revenue) have to say. They may even want to influence your editorial vision. In other words, if the company selling lipstick is going to pay you to put their ad on your blog, they may not want you writing about how great it is to go out without makeup on. You get the idea. When commerce meets art, art can get compromised. This doesn't mean you need to hold your editorial vision hostage to the mighty dollar. You'll find your own line that defines where you will or won't compromise. It's a personal decision, and as long as you're aware of the potential for conflict of interest, you'll be able to navigate the challenges.

The same goes for your photography business. You may love taking candid, lyrical photos of your subject, but maybe your first couple of clients are schools that need kids sitting in chairs on picture day. Do you turn down the business and stick to your artistic aesthetic, or do you say yes to the dollar and take the pictures the way your client wants them?

BEING PAID TO BE AN ARTIST IN ANY FORM CAN INVOLVE COMPROMISE AT TIMES, but you don't have to feel like you're selling out just because an editor has opinions or a client thinks they know more about musical interludes than you do. You can do both the art you love and the art you do as a business, creating work that is just your own as well as pieces commissioned by your clients.

Remember that everyone who pursues an artistic endeavor goes through what you're experiencing. So share your successes and your failures with fellow artists who get it. They will remind you that pursuing an artistic talent requires hard work and a constant willingness to put yourself—and your art—out there for others to see and judge and evaluate. You need to develop a thick skin and a willingness to keep at it for as long as it takes.

As a musician making her living in New York City, Alyson Greenfield has had to learn the art of compromise.

◇◇

ALYSON

Being a dreamer is a really beautiful thing—you do need a little bit of head-in-the-clouds, you need to see something that doesn't exist. Sometimes that quality helped me execute the things I've done because I'm open. But people don't understand—talent is only a part of success. There are so many more components. Even if you don't get to the level of where you think you should or want to, it's not about your level of talent. In New York City, where I live, there are more talented musicians than you could even deal with. Most people don't know who they are. It's not because they're not good. There's an industry and commerce, and it's hard.

YOU ARE NOT YOUR STARTUP

This is a good place to talk about the difference between *you* and that thing you're creating. On the surface it sounds obvious, but think about it: your product is more than just what goes in the box or bag—it's a part of you. It's something close to your heart that you're putting out there for other people to consume. That's true whether you're making buttercream frosting or writing a novel. You've put a lot of yourself into creating something. You'd like other people to want it. You'd like them to buy it. And sometimes it can hurt if they don't.

IT'S EASY TO GET STUCK IN THE WHAT-IFS. What if no one wants to buy my knitted scarves? What if someone thinks I have no talent? What if I'm not as creative and talented as I'd like to believe?

You can only get so much mileage from self-doubt. It's good to have a bit of it, to keep your ego from ballooning. But after that dose, let the rest go. Don't let your fears stop you from stepping out the door with your fabulous new lines of code or letting someone read your poems. We all go through moments of self-doubt, but you need to separate the fear and self-consciousness from the creation itself. Let your talent and drive—and your gorgeous knitted scarves, your cool dangling earrings, or your innovative game design—speak for themselves.

ALWAYS REMEMBER THAT YOU ARE A PERSON WITH MANY FABULOUS ATTRIBUTES, CREATIVITY, VISION, AND GUTSINESS. Even if an idea is not successful, it doesn't mean you are not successful. And if one product goes off the charts, it doesn't mean that your creative self is a lucky one-hit wonder who will never have that kind of success again. You and your abilities and your determination—those are things that don't change with the ebb and flow of business. Your ideas and your creations come from you but they *aren't* you. They don't define you and your abilities, so don't let them take on more importance than they deserve. Hard work and perseverance matter more than raw talent.

BRAND IT!

Before you present your creation to the world, think about how to make a great first impression. The look and feel of your product has to be unique to you. Let's say your avid snowboarding revealed a need for attractive, super warm bandannas and you've created three dozen from soft fleece. Now you want to package them up and get people to buy them. You need to have a vision for your brand—a unique presentation that attracts potential buyers.

THREE RULES OF THUMB

CONSISTENCY: When people buy your bandannas, they should be confident of getting the same great design and warmth every time. Think about why a company like Starbucks is so successful: you can go into any Starbucks in any city and have an identical experience. There's a feeling of comfort your customer gets from knowing that every time they put on your product, they're in for a toasty ride on their board. Don't suddenly change to an itchy wool blend or use cheaper fleece that might be irritating.

ACCESSIBILITY: Don't hide your snowboarding bandannas in sealed-up white boxes where people can only imagine how great they look. Make use of cellophane wrapping or display the bandannas in baskets. People buy things because they look enticing. They can imagine themselves wearing the necklace they see hanging by the cash register. They can imagine the taste of that scone when they see the blueberries peeking out from its browned and sugared crust. Again, think about Starbucks. Do you think it's an accident that you have to stand in front of the cake pops and butter croissants while you're waiting to order, and that those delicious-looking desserts are right at eye level? The whole time you're waiting to order your coffee, you're ogling the baked goods, which are beautifully displayed on ceramic plates under flattering lights. You can use the same tricks of the trade. Don't obscure your product's appeal by hiding it. Let it sell itself.

IMAGE: Cool packaging and an intriguing logo can give your product a whole other dimension. Here's where your creativity really pays off. Make up an appealing, unique name for your business. Sprinkles Cupcakes started a revolution. Cupcakes were a boring birthday party staple when Candace Nelson started baking. She created flavors no one had seen, intrigued customers with a cupcake vending machine outside the store, and redefined the industry. People lined up out the door because she created a must-have dessert with a creative name. Cupcakes, which had been generic supermarket treats, now had special cachet when they came in a Sprinkles box.

MAKE IT SUSTAINABLE FOR YOU RIGHT NOW

The number one rule for launching something that will succeed is making it something you can work into your life. If you're taking a full classload and playing two club sports and an instrument, you may not have the bandwidth for the startup of your dreams right now. That's okay. You can still get started.

BE REALISTIC about how much time you can devote to something, but don't let fear of not having enough time hold you back. Find some way to fit in what you want to do. If that means taking a break during the school year and going full bore into a project in the summer, do that. Or if it means asking a friend or family member to help you carry the load, consider whether you can share the burden. Not everything has to get done right away. All of our Bosses who've worked on their ventures while in school faced those challenges. They figured out ways to get things done and still keep their grades up. Sometimes it feels like a trade-off, but that's the life of a student. It's a tremendous balancing act, and you can handle it.

Deepika Bodapati faced this challenge in her high school and college years while devising science fair projects with real-world applications, which eventually led to her cofounding a company that developed a successful portable blood-screening device.

◇◇◇

DEEPIKA

Managing flying back and forth with school is hard. Before, I used to spend a whole day doing a lab. Now, if I'm lucky, I get do it on the airplane or in the hour after I come back before I go to sleep so I can turn it in the next day. It's not difficult work, but it's hard to manage it all. When you're working on something you're so excited about, it's fine when things are good, but when things are bad, all you want to do is work on the project. I'm always wanting to do that. There's always something to be done. It's all about moving fast, and that's been that hardest part.

You have to be aware that time you're spending at school is time that's going to make a dent in the work. Time you're not spending on schoolwork is going to make a dent there.

REVISE AND REFINE

The idea you start with may not be exactly what you end up with. Starting anything is a process of seeing what works and what doesn't. The beauty of starting small and launching in your own backyard is that you're free to shake out the mistakes and redirect yourself. Your business may also need to change and adapt over time—what worked at the beginning might not always be the best way to run things.

Niharika Bedekar founded her organization, Power Up, while she was still in high school. As she got older and changed, Power Up began to evolve accordingly.

NIHARIKA

Once I got to college, I realized a lot of the work [I was doing] in high school had been me in person talking to girls, Girls Scouts—me giving curriculum. As I get older, that's going to be a less sustainable model. Now I'm looking at how I can best use lessons I learned from things that worked very well to build something more sustainable. I am a huge supporter of the power of storytelling. I want to talk to people, to young girls, and tell them everything's going to be okay as they go through puberty. It's a weird, scary process but everyone in nature has been through it. There's a collective support group.

JUST ONE MORE THING

It's entirely possible that you're not ready to start something just yet. Not everyone has a startup on the brain or an app ready to manufacture—at least not yet. Does that mean you need to stop reading now and hope for inspiration at a later date? No.

Start now by doing something that brings you closer to what you might like to do. Even if you're not ready to launch something of your own, start collecting information and getting acquainted with what's out there in different industries. Internships or summer jobs are a great way to do that, as are classes or community service projects after school. Think big, but always be willing to do small jobs or internships that may seem slightly far afield of what you want to be doing. They can give you great skills, or turn into a bigger job, or set you going on a direction that could change your life. Finding the right internship can be as simple as searching for something that interests you on internships.com, which sources interning opportunities across diverse industries all over the country. You can also get very specific and look at the Careers section of most companies' websites, where they'll post both paid and unpaid opportunities, along with descriptions of the qualities they're looking for in an applicant. So if you're a coder who loves playing video games, you can look at the job listings at a company like Riot Games or check the job board in the engineering department of a nearby college for postings for people with your skill set.

Chelsea Siler took this "just get started" route to her eventual position as senior communications officer for the Canadian Broadcasting Company/Radio Canada, as well as owner of her own public relations and marketing firm.

◇◇

CHELSEA

I took a job I knew I wouldn't like, working for an oil and gas company. I knew it was just a job, a paycheck coming in. But at the same time, I opened my own company. I registered a business, got a sales tax number. I would take meetings outside regular work hours. I kept my skills up outside of work and took freelance contracts in the evenings and on weekends.

I'd ask friends of friends, "Do you need a contract to be done?" This was a business that was me, something that I had control over, and I was pleasantly surprised with the amount of work I got. I still have the business, called Five & Vine, and I do freelance work in public relations, communications, media service, business plans, and social media plans.

High school internships set Neeka Mashouf on her way to her present work as a builder of the solar car and founder of a startup aimed at providing renewable energy to people worldwide who don't have access to electricity.

NEEKA

I had some cool opportunities when I was in high school to do some really awesome internships. I was always interested in science and engineering. My first internship was in an algae biofuel startup company. I was working in a lab developing biofuels with my hands deep in green, slimy, gross algae. I saw that the CEOs had an idea of biofuel that would change the world. Working there, I could totally see myself doing something like that.

The next internship in high school was working at Lawrence Berkeley National Lab developing materials for artificial photosynthesis. I developed a material that would take sunlight and split it with water and develop hydrogen gas to develop fuel for fuel cells. The hands-on experience I got working on world-changing technology was amazing. I learned that anyone can create change and shape the future and develop cool things they're passionate about. The people I worked with were superpassionate and wanted to improve the world. And they were doing it.

"I'VE COME TO BELIEVE THAT EACH OF US HAS A PERSONAL CALLING THAT'S AS UNIQUE AS A FINGERPRINT—AND THAT THE BEST WAY TO SUCCEED IS TO DISCOVER WHAT YOU LOVE AND THEN FIND A WAY TO OFFER IT TO OTHERS IN THE FORM OF SERVICE, WORKING HARD, AND ALSO ALLOWING THE ENERGY OF THE UNIVERSE TO LEAD YOU."

—Oprah Winfrey, media icon and entrepreneur

CHAPTER 4

IDEA STARTUPS

ALSO KNOWN AS SERVICE BUSINESSES

If you are in an idea or service business—politics, web design, green business consulting, math tutoring, style makeovers, performing—the thing you're selling is a service: something you can do for someone else. Sometimes the thing you're selling feels like a more obvious business, like painting murals or taking photos of events. Other times, you may wonder whether the political blog you write daily or the judo program you started for at-risk teens even counts as a business. Yes, it does.

SERVICES OR IDEA BUSINESSES OFTEN HAVE LOW STARTUP COSTS. Unlike goods-based businesses, you don't have to buy a bunch of supplies or equipment, A portable bicycle maker would need wheels, metal, and tools. A stationery maker might need a letterpress and reams of paper and ink. A writer, however, whether she is starting a blog or writing a series of short stories that will one day make up a book needs only time and her ideas. A consultant, perhaps one who offers bedroom design services, or a designer who makes web pages or creates custom logos just needs a computer, a place to work, and maybe some software.

SOME SERVICE BUSINESSES DO REQUIRE EQUIPMENT. If you are an event photographer, you'll need a camera. If you have a car-detailing business, you'll need soap, wax, and buckets. But, in general, you're providing help to someone else. People will hire you if you can do the work better than they can do it themselves, or if they're just too busy to do it. You'll need to show them samples or a list of services, but the service you're providing is something you know how to do.

AN IDEA BUSINESS STARTS WITH AN IDEA *YOU* LIKE. Think about your skills and what you enjoy. Writing or designing, for example: You can be a blogger, a web designer, a freelance article writer, or a graphic artist. Your skills may seem obvious to you, but just because you find it easy and fun to carve an elaborate Halloween pumpkin doesn't mean it's easy for everyone. Lots of people can't write, or draw, or understand technology. If you have these skills, you can do work for other people. What better business is there? Corvida Raven started online tech newsletter shegeeks.net to translate the latest trends in technology into plain words we can all understand. It was a simple concept that grew into a huge success.

WHAT KIND OF SERVICE BUSINESS CAN YOU START? Begin by thinking like a busy person. What are the top five things a busy person has no time to do? Run errands? Perfect. You can start a business being a personal assistant or an errand runner. If you have a car or bike, you can offer to pick up dry cleaning, do grocery shopping, or buy birthday gifts. Voilá: a business is born.

We all try to multitask, but things have a way of creeping onto our to-do lists and staying there for a long time. What else might a busy person need help getting done? Walking the dog, cooking balanced dinners, driving kids to sports practices? That's how Blue Apron and TaskRabbit were born. You can turn other people's needs into your business ideas.

SELL YOUR SERVICE. Idea businesses have the challenge of selling something that isn't tangible. Sometimes they require more explanation, like a slideshow presentation or a short video to show people how they work. When you introduce people to your service, make sure they understand exactly what you can do for them and why they should hire you. To grow a service business you may need to focus more on marketing efforts to make your service feel like a product.

Juliette Brindak Blake was just 13 when she created her idea business,
Miss O and Friends, a safe social media site for tween girls.

◇◇◇

JULIETTE

When it first started, it wasn't a business. The characters of the Miss O
girls started off as my drawings. It was basically a hobby that my mom,
my sister, Olivia, and I did. Then, for Olivia's eighth birthday, my mom and
I made Miss O characters for all of my sister's friends and they went crazy.
They loved them. I was 13 at the time, my sister was 8, and that's the time
when things start to get a little bit rough for girls. There are cliques at school,
along with changes physically and emotionally. It's just really stressful. So,
I thought, we should really start doing something for these girls.

ARE YOU A HYBRID?

DO YOU HAVE A BUSINESS THAT COMBINES SEVERAL THINGS? Many businesses have a goods component and a services component. You may start by making watercolor paintings with sports themes for kids' bedrooms, but you may later decide to create a line of stationery and thank-you notes with your designs. A photographer might sell coffee table books. A YouTuber may create how-to videos and produce a web series.

Think about offshoot products that may support your business and provide extra revenues. You don't have to pursue them now, but part of thinking big is allowing yourself to take interesting paths if they open up, following up on new opportunities, and thinking about where you'll go once you've met the goals you set now.

When Deepika Bodapati and her partner first started their company, Athelas, they were creating a product that performed a service. That gave them a toe in both worlds, where they'd need to refine the specifications of the product itself while making sure to explain how it could serve doctors and entire communities.

DEEPIKA

Athelas is a blood analytic company that leverages computer vision and machine learning to characterize blood and spit out a diagnostic. We eclipsed a 24-hour process. When you're sick and a nurse checks your vitals like your heart rate, the nurse pricks your finger and puts our test strip next to it to suck up some blood. The strip then gets inserted into the hardware, and a back-end algorithm will use a camera to take a bunch of snapshots so we get multiple fields of view. We can characterize that sample so we can spit out a diagnostic. The cartridge has an automated system to analyze the contents of the blood sample. It's computer vision-based hardware instead of chemical-based hardware.

With one drop of blood you can determine what a person is facing. It's like a thermometer, one of the first lines of defense. We can equip doctors with this strip. Even a quick read increases what they can do in an appointment: determine allergic reactions, look for bacterial infections, viral infections, mono, anemia, sickle cell anemia, leukemia.

FIND YOUR NICHE

You are powerful and motivated, but even you can't be all things to all people all the time. The better you know yourself and the more specialized the service you offer, the easier it is to tell a future client or booking agent or potential source of funds what you do. You don't have to specialize right away.

> *At age 23, Alex Douwes and Nellie Morris founded Purpose Generation, a consulting firm to teach businesses how to reach millennials.*

◇◇

NELLIE AND ALEX

In the beginning, we took on every possible project, even if it had nothing to do with our target audience. We certainly learned a lot in the process, but it was hard to stay focused or scale because we kept following every shiny penny. As soon as we defined what we do and, more important, what we don't do, we took off. Now we have a much tighter pitch and can focus on what we do best.

DO YOU HAVE TO MAKE MONEY TO BE A STARTUP BUSINESS? NOPE.

Businesses that are not in the business of generating profits are called, aptly enough, nonprofits. Nonprofit businesses need to generate only enough funds to operate and by definition don't have anything left over. Nonprofits are eligible to apply for grant money (while for-profit businesses are not), which means people and organizations who give money get a tax break for doing so and therefore have a greater incentive for helping you out. There are many organizations, large and small, that provide money for nonprofits. The downside is that there are a lot of organizations competing for that money.

It's best to start with local foundations that donate to organizations in your field. Start with grants.gov or an internet search for specific organizations that offer grant money and the requirements for applying.

To take donations, your nonprofit needs to be established as a corporation, which will give it a tax ID number and tax-exempt status. You'll also need to set up a bank account, so you'll be able to deposit the funds you receive. There are lots of online resources that explain the process.

Priscilla Guo went to local government to start up her nonprofit program teaching computer coding to low-income middle school students in Harlem.

◇◇◇

PRISCILLA

It's really important for me to give back in the future. When I blogged on education reform for the New York Campaign for Achievement Now (NYCAN), I was astounded by the statistics I found on how many people do not have access to computer science courses or are digitally illiterate in New York alone. In 2013, I testified about the issue at the New York City interagency coordinating council meeting, and my proposal to institute a computer coding program for middle school students was approved by Jeanne Mullgrav, commissioner of New York City's Department of Youth and Community Development. I began this program, called NYC TechY, in Harlem in the summer of 2014, and each summer I teach students the basics of computer programming and technical skills. The program has been so successful that it has now been expanded to Ravenswood in western Queens.

My first year, I took the students to Google for a company visit and tour. They were in awe—people have this as a career? They were telling me that the only people they saw leading successful lives, who looked like them, were in the music industry or making it big in sports. If you don't expose kids to a diverse set of potential careers, they don't have the pathways for success. My students had so many ideas about mobile applications they wanted to build and digital tools they wanted to create. After seeing a tech career firsthand, they were motivated to continue their studies in computer science. We need their perspectives in the tech industry, because they can begin to solve some of the world's hardest problems.

PUBLIC SERVICE

PUBLIC SERVICE ESSENTIALLY MEANS HELPING OTHERS. There are many ways to do that. Some large companies build capitalist dreams and then set aside money for foundations that fund research and help people in need. The Bill Gates Foundation is one of the biggest, having donated over $36 billion since it was launched in 2000. Think of ways you'd like to give back, even while your business is small, such as donating a percentage of your sales to a worthy cause.

You can also build a project or venture around public service right now. Nonprofit organizations take money raised through donations and pour them directly into helping others. Whether that means starting a winter coat drive or creating a community food garden, your startup can be built on the mission of helping others.

After learning that in rural Zimbabwe, it rained only a couple of months out of the year and that the women struggled to grow staple foods in the drier seasons, Naama Raz-Yaseef used her skills as an eco-hydrologist to developed a simple, affordable mobile irrigation system that allowed these women to water their crops year-round.

NAAMA

In my primary work, I had focused on eco-hydrology, which looks at how water is redistributed in the ecosystem. I'd look at rain: Where does it go? Who uses it first? How is it redistributed in the ecosystem? I would try to understand what will happen in the future. I would go back to the laboratory and analyze data. I thought of my work as being an environmental psychologist—like a therapist—because I was trying to understand what matters to the ecosystem.

I'd been doing this for years but felt like it wasn't enough. I needed to do something that connected me more to communities, to people. I felt a desire to utilize my expertise and do something good with it.

JUST ONE MORE THING

JUST BECAUSE SOMETHING IS HARD DOESN'T MEAN YOU'RE DOING IT WRONG. It's going to get challenging. There will be days when you're not sure it's worth it, days when you think it might just be easier to work for someone else, build someone else's dream, let that person take the risk and get beaten down. We all have moments of doubt and days we'd rather not relive. Sometimes the yield from the hardest days is the very thing that propels you forward the next day. Getting started is rarely glamorous. It's about taking the first steps and moving forward toward your goal.

Debbie Fung was 23 when she and her partner founded Yoga Tree, a yoga studio in Toronto, Canada. After an inauspicious beginning, nine years later she co-owns five yoga studios and has plans to open five more.

DEBBIE

Our first day in December 2007 was a snowfall day. We offered free yoga: 8 classes, and 11 people showed up. It was sad. We decided it was okay. We then thought, We have to get to work. We were in for a five-year lease. So we decided to offer free yoga for an entire month. We understood that in our area it's not just because it was a snowy day. It was Hanukkah and people were out of town. We ended up extending our offering to two or three months of yoga. People were saying, "Why would you do this?" Our drive was not financial. We knew this would go somewhere.

We had no sales for the first week or the second week. In January, we hadn't made enough to pay our rent or our instructors. On the twenty-ninth day of January, we had extended hours. We called back everyone who had taken a free class. We were in sales mode until twelve at night. If you give your heart to a business, people will see you're doing something great for the community and appreciate that.

KEEP IT SIMPLE

In other words, don't drive yourself crazy.

Remember, none of us can do everything. So don't try to run a floral design business by growing the flowers yourself and weaving your own baskets. Learn where it makes sense to have others do some legwork for you, so you can focus on what you do best, arranging the blooms into beautiful designs and creating unusual combinations of plants. Working this way doesn't mean you're being lazy. You're being efficient.

People have limited time to size up what you're doing and decide whether they need it or not. Keep your concept clean and don't make them work too hard. Remember what you do best and do that one thing.

SUCCESSFUL SERVICE BUSINESSES

THAT DO SOMETHING REALLY SIMPLE

AMAZON—Billed as earth's biggest bookstore, Amazon sells a whole lot more. But really, they don't make anything. They get what you want from a huge variety of sources and ship it to you.

EBAY—You can find pretty much anything you want on eBay. They just connect buyers with sellers, a service.

DRYBAR—They have products, too, like blow-dryers, shampoos, and brushes, but Drybar's main business is drying your hair so you don't have to.

SOULCYCLE—They're selling sweat: yours. Sure, they have bikes and a place to use them, but they're basically offering a service: an instructor to guide you through a ride. You do the work. They just give you the setup.

"WHEN I DARE TO BE POWERFUL, TO USE MY STRENGTH IN THE SERVICE OF MY VISION, THEN IT BECOMES LESS AND LESS IMPORTANT WHETHER I AM AFRAID."

—Audre Lorde, writer and activist

CHAPTER 5

YOU ARE YOUNG AND FEMALE

➤ TIME TO OWN IT ◀

The whole point of being young and female and having great ideas is that you've got a fire burning that isn't going to be put out by the flame of someone skeptical. So what if someone thinks you're too young to have a startup? So what if someone says girls can't do that? It will take you all of a minute to prove that person wrong if you're prepared with your business sense, your drive, and your passion for your ideas.

There will be times it feels like being young is a rock you have to push up a big hill every time you go out and try to talk to someone about your startup. We've all experienced the look of shock on someone's face when it turned out we really do have something great to say. Now's the time to prove all the naysayers wrong.

YOUNG + FEMALE = AWESOME!

SOMETIMES YOU HAVE TO REMIND YOURSELF OF THAT. The people you're meeting with when you're getting your venture off the ground might not always believe you can do everything you know you can do, but you are there to convince them. Don't let your age or gender or someone else's idea of what you should be determine your sense of self—or your future. Young and female? Face it head-on and let people know that being young means you have fresh ideas and energy. Being female means you're tough and you don't give up. You're Boss. You know what to do.

WE STILL LIVE IN A WORLD WHERE WE LACK GENDER EQUALITY IN MOST FIELDS. Women make up half the workforce, but represent only 25% in the fields of science, technology, engineering, and math. Nearly one-third of practicing physicians are women, with just over one-third working as full-time medical faculty, according to the American Association of Medical Colleges. And a study by the Center for the Study of Women in Television and Film at San Diego State University found that women make up just 7% of directors of the top 250 films and 13% of writers on the top 700 films. The 2016 Fortune 500 CEOs included only 21 women, which works out to just over 4%. The numbers can feel discouraging, but look at them as a yardstick for where we are and where we still need to go.

Here's what our Bosses have to say about it.

JULIETTE (MISS O AND FRIENDS)

I'm a member of lots of different entrepreneurial organizations, and I'll always be introduced as "This is Juliette Brindak, she's a young female entrepreneur who has a website where girls can play games." And it bothers me so much because there's a guy who's also my age who also has some other kind of website or product, but I'm the "young female." They're not introducing him as a young male. Hello, I am young and I am female and you don't have to point out the obvious. It's one of the things I really can't stand.

When I would present to Colgate, Procter & Gamble, Yahoo, or Target, they would be shocked that a 16-year-old could present a company to them. I think that they were really impressed. I knew the brand, I knew what we were trying to do, and they couldn't really tell me otherwise because they didn't know, and it was me telling them.

ALEX AND NELLIE (PURPOSE GENERATION)

We were 23 when we started the company with little credibility and track record. We realized early on that the key to acquiring new business was getting buy-in from the highest executive levels. We worked incredibly hard to prove ourselves to those first few clients who took a chance on us. We spent our first two years heads-down, focused on delivering better outcomes than any of our competitors. As a result, most of our growth has been the result of word of mouth and referrals, something we're very proud of.

Millennials wasn't a buzzword when we started. Instead of hiding our age, we used it to our advantage and pitched clients on the need for a "millennial tour guide" to help them identify the right trends, environments, networks, and partners to connect with. We turned a perceived weakness into a strength and made it the core of our pitch.

Confidence is a very important character trait to develop, especially for entrepreneurs. Yet millennials sometimes get a bad rap for being overconfident. We never assume that we have the answer—or that there's only one right answer for that matter—but we're confident we can get you the answer by asking the right questions and talking to the right people.

GABRIELLE (JEWELZ OF JORDAN)

I know a lot of people might think you should start a career as an adult, but I think it's good to start something at a young age. First, you have more time to make mistakes and more time for learning. You don't have to be an entrepreneur in the future if you don't want, but if you want to be a mechanical engineer or create an app, start now. I want to be a gemologist, so I'm taking classes on that now because I have more time to learn, more time to develop. You can become an expert in a certain field and be ahead of the game. You have more time to create and to grow.

DEBBIE (YOGA TREE)

At 23 people didn't take us seriously and were concerned about buying a membership with us. They'd ask: "Will these two young people run away with our membership money? "How long do think you'll be in business for?" "Where's your family from?"

CHENTAL-SONG (HONEY BUNCH KIDS)

My age has definitely been a factor. When I first started I was 13, and people thought it was so cute that this little teenager was promoting her own books. Now I'm almost 20, and when people hear I've been working on this almost 10 years, they take it more seriously because I've been doing it for such a long time.

PRISCILLA (NYC TECHY)

One of my concerns is fighting for equality in the workplace. I've had experiences working in a male-dominated industry, and those experiences have prepared me to assert myself in the workplace. How do you take ownership of your idea? You have to practice. In all my meetings, I find that it's not about being the loudest one in the room, but about being confident in what you're saying. Don't qualify your statements with

"I think" or "maybe." I've seen too many men take credit for a woman's idea. Represent yourself and be confident in your ideas, because your input is valued.

In my courses on the history of computing, I've learned that the gender imbalance in the technology industry was largely socially engineered. Sixty years ago, women were dominating the field. Now we only hear about the "founding fathers" of Silicon Valley, as *Newsweek* termed them. In fact, the mother of software, Ada Lovelace, in the nineteenth century conceived a vision of what computing is now. And Rear Admiral Grace Hopper invented the first compiler for a computer programming language on the Harvard Mark I. Then, in the mid-twentieth century, we see advertisements of women who are portrayed to be "too emotional" in the workplace. There are even ads that suggest that women's nails would scratch the computer tape and serve as a hindrance to computing work. We must look at the history because it can inform us of our modern-day shortcomings. We must recognize that women can do anything that they put their minds to.

CHARLOTTE (FE MAIDENS)

Women are still a massive minority within the STEM community. Prejudice is a major inhibition: many women are still overlooked and underestimated, both professionally and personally. Although sexism against women in science is no secret, people tend to undervalue how common it is. Members of our team often face discriminating comments and behavior at robotics competitions, from students making generalizations about us to judges objectifying or disparaging us.

"POWER'S NOT GIVEN TO YOU.
YOU HAVE TO TAKE IT. "

—Beyoncé Knowles-Carter, singer-songwriter and businesswoman

CHAPTER 6

YOUR BRAND

t's time to put your mark on the world. You need to think about everything you do in terms of building recognition for your business. In other words, build a brand: make people associate your business with you. The image you put out to the world every time you have a public conversation, every time you post something online, is the image your business will share. That means you should think before you speak. It means you should be positive even if you're feeling down. If you tweet snarky things, people might not be able to distinguish your humor from the business you're running. That doesn't mean you can't have fun—it just means that your fun reflects on your business, so be conscious of how you express yourself.

YOU'VE ALREADY BEEN BUILDING A BRAND FOR YEARS. If you've established a regular presence on Facebook, Instagram, Twitter, Snapchat, Tumblr, or whichever social media site works for you, you've been building a brand: you *are* the brand. Everything you post or tweet or say is furthering the image you put forth to the world. You may not have realized it, but you probably have some habits. We all do. Some of us like to post pictures of athletics: teams we play on, races we've run, photos wearing finishers' medals, logos of our favorite teams. Some of us post information about music: where our band is playing, record release information, videos of performances. Friends start looking forward to the posts; next thing we know, we've got followers— maybe lots of them.

You may be someone who regularly posts information about fitness. Or service learning opportunities. Maybe you went from posting pictures of great omelets you made in your kitchen to posting recipes for gorgeous desserts. Pretty soon your friends or followers are taking note of the recipes and making them too. Maybe your incredible snapshots of the beach cleanup you do every weekend has motivated your friends to join in, and now you've started a movement. You've developed a reputation. Your followers comment and their friends start wanting to follow you too. This is true whether you regularly post about art or urban renewal or opinions on politics. The more you post, the more those friends and followers begin to expect that consistency, checking your feeds for a regular dose of what they've come to enjoy.

ALL THIS MEANS YOU ARE ALREADY AN EXPERT AT BRANDING even if you don't know it. You have already developed an identity. Now's the time to transfer that know-how to your business.

> ## EXAMPLES OF BUSINESSES
> ### WITH GREAT BRAND IDENTITY
>
> * **NIKE**—You see the swoosh and you think Nike: sports, shoes, speed. Even their tagline, "Just Do It," remains front of mind once you've seen it.
>
> * **APPLE**—If you google "apple," the first search item that appears is not the fruit, even though the average American eats 50 pounds of apples a year. The first item is Apple computer, which has done a splendid job of marrying its name with its products.
>
> * **MCDONALD'S**—The ubiquitous golden arches are recognized all around the world, and everyone knows their commercial jingle "I'm Lovin' It."

NAME IT

COME UP WITH A GOOD NAME. Your new venture needs a name that gets people's attention. Make a list: write down every name that comes to mind when you think of the kind of venture you have. If you're a singer, actor, writer, or any other version of an artist, you may want to choose a stage or pen name. Be creative: as long as it feels like you, there's no wrong name at this point.

Next, ask for opinions on your ideas for names or taglines. You can even design an opinion poll on SurveyMonkey.com and ask what your friends think about your concept, name, and idea. Research, compare, and then decide on your business name. Make sure you love it.

DESIGN IT

THERE'S THE VISUAL PART OF YOUR BRAND, TOO. A logo is a visual representation that makes people think of your business every time they see it. There are companies that specialize in building brands and developing identifiable logo designs. However, you don't need to invest thousands in brand consultants—you just need to understand what they're doing and why. Then you need to do it yourself.

They key is to develop a combination of typestyle, design, and colors that is iconic and synonymous with your product, so that even if someone didn't see the name, they'd know what it was. Take the Twitter bird. It was such a simple design concept, but it quickly became both an identifiable logo and an icon for tweeting itself.

START BY LOOKING AROUND AT LOGOS YOU LIKE. All companies have them, even if they don't make a product. Think about font styles. Everybody recognizes the font used by Facebook: the lowercase *f*, the rounded letters. Even if you just saw that blue *f*, you'd know it was Facebook, right? Or think about the sleeker font used by YouTube. The red-box background behind the word *Tube* and the way the two words are smashed together—none of that is accidental. Companies spend lots of time trying out different types of lettering and different designs until they land on something that evokes their brands.

WHEN YOU'RE THINKING ABOUT FONTS AND LETTERING, keep in mind the kind of business you have and the kind of image you want to present. If you are making a product aimed at kids, you might like to use a font that looks playful and is easy to read. If you want a retro feel, you might choose one that evokes the 1920s or the old West. Fancy scripted letters don't necessarily say "car detailing business." And big clunky letters would seem odd if you are marketing yourself as someone who does fine calligraphy and decoration on invitations. Be consistent. Use the font to communicate something about your business. It's an opportunity for you to send a message without saying a word.

NOW FOR THE ACTUAL DESIGN. Keep it simple. Maybe you just need the first letter of your business name enlarged in a color you like with a small doodle. Maybe you don't need the doodle. You just need something eye catching and easily identified with you and your business. Even if you don't consider yourself an artist, you can still come up with a great design—it doesn't have to be complicated. If you pull an image from the internet, make sure you're not violating copyright rules. Someone designed that piece of art, and while a lot of images are in the public domain, meaning that anyone is free to use them, some images are not. Often you will find a notation on an image explaining who owns the copyright. Reach out and request their permission to use it. Or let it be your starting point for coming up with something new.

DANGER AHEAD!
DESIGN FLAWS TO AVOID

* Too busy: are you inducing vertigo with your kitschy-flowery-punk package design?

* Don't let your design compete with your product.

* Don't choose packaging that costs so much that it's taking a big bite out of profits.

* Are you going for such safe colors and designs that no one will notice you in a crowd?

* Is there a chance your product will be confused with someone else's?

FINISH YOUR LOGO

ADD ART. OR NOT. Does your logo need an illustration to get your identity across? You will need to find a graphic artist or illustrator.

WHEN YOU SIT DOWN TO GET STARTED WITH YOUR ARTIST, BE SPECIFIC. Look around for images you especially like. Do you like literal designs—a dog in a bed for a maker of dog beds—or abstract art that looks cool and a little mysterious? Bring in samples and photos of what you like, and make sure to mention any colors like or you really can't stand. Then let the artist get creative.

It's exciting to see your idea come to life in the form of an image. Remember that you don't need to settle for the first drawing or idea that's presented to you. Ask for a few variations and then conduct a little informal poll, or even crowdsource on your Instagram and ask people to pick which they like best and tell you why. The "why" part is important because it will force you and anyone who looks at your logo to look a little harder and really figure out what's working and what isn't.

AFTER YOU CHOOSE YOUR LOGO, USE IT LIKE CRAZY. Get a big roll of stickers made so you can put them on packaging and envelopes. Put the logo on your website. Get business cards made—you can order them online for pennies—and the first time you hand one out, you'll feel so official. The first time someone uses your business card to contact you for a job, you'll feel awesome. Begin the process of getting people to associate your logo with your business and all the great things you're doing.

PACKAGING

An eggshell is not only a convenient storage device for an egg—it's an ingenious packaging solution, both functional and attractive. Packaging isn't just a utilitarian proposition. It has feel, functionality, and a look that reflects your brand and will distinguish your product from the next thing over on the shelf.

There's a reason cereal comes in a box with pictures of the cereal on the front: **PEOPLE WANT TO KNOW WHAT THEY'RE BUYING.** If that same cereal were packaged in foil or in a box without a photo, it wouldn't sell as well. Keep this in mind when you're figuring out packaging for your goods. If you're making soft felt hats, package them minimally— maybe with just a cool

COLORS SEND MESSAGES

* **BLUE** appeals to men and women, one reason why it's a common color in packaging and design.

* **RED** is dominant and energetic, great for grabbing attention, and studies show it actually makes people hungrier. That's why lots of fast-food restaurants have red in their logos.

* **GREEN** says "fresh and natural." It can also signify an environmentally friendly business.

* Lots of people associate the color **PINK** with women, so guys might think the product's not for them if you use this color. This might be exactly what you want, but it might not!

* **YELLOW** makes people happy.

* **BROWN** can feel earthy, especially if you're using unbleached paper instead of white.

logo tag hanging off or a cardboard band to keep the hat folded up. Let people touch and see how soft the felt is and how cute your designs are.

If you're selling something with lots of pieces and parts, you'll do well to keep everything organized in a bag or box, maybe separated within by smaller compartments, or lettered or numbered. Be sure to include clear, accurate instructions. How many times have you bought something only to wonder if they're talking about the big nail or the medium-size nail when they're telling you to hammer the thing together? Make your pieces easy to sort out and put together.

None of this means you have to invest a ton in packaging materials. Craft shops and office or restaurant supply stores have all sorts of efficient, generic packaging in bulk. It's clean looking, and by adding a sticker with your logo, you've created perfect personalized packaging.

BRAND AWARENESS

Now that you have a product, a business name, and a logo, you are on your way to building your brand. And remember that when we refer to things like "your product," we're not only talking about things like shoes or scarves or pencil cases. Your product is your voice if you are a singer, it's your writing if you're a writer, it's your service if you have chosen a service business.

You can create awareness for your brand all over the place. Think about all the locations, both in the physical world and the digital one, where you can promote your brand, from posting flyers on notice boards to posting online.

MAKE EVERY INTERACTION MEMORABLE

When it's time to deliver your product to customers, present it well. Wrap it in nice paper and include a thank-you note. Sponge-print some butcher paper and use it to stuff boxes. Buy tissue paper in bulk to wrap what you're sending and use one of your cute logo stickers to seal it. Enclose your business card with a handwritten "thanks" at the bottom. You'd be surprised how much these personal touches influence people. Leaving your customers with a positive feeling will make them want to come back to you.

If you e-mail receipts for transactions, make them friendly. Put your logo in your e-mail signature and on everything associated with your business.

Consider using a photo of yourself in your catalog or on your website—people like to know who they're dealing with. Showing them who you are will go a long way toward making your customer feel a more personal relationship with your company.

TEN WAYS TO BUILD BRAND AWARENESS

~~~~~~~~~~~~~~~~

1. **BUSINESS CARDS**—They're easy to print up yourself or order online. You can find templates in word processing programs and print them on card stock at an office supply store. Business phone and e-mail contact information is plenty. Keep a handful of cards with you all the time. When you're having a conversation about your business and someone asks how to get in touch with you, pull out a card.

2. **FLIERS/POSTCARDS**—You can print these up yourself, too. Fliers are great for advertising local services or announcing an event at which you'll be selling or performing. Ask local businesses if they're willing to post your flier or stack up your postcards.

3. **SOCIAL MEDIA POSTS**—Just the way you'd post an update on which concert you went to over the weekend, you should post updates on your business: gigs you're playing, craft fairs where you'll be selling, a new flavor you've perfected. Let people know. Update often.

4. **TWEETS**—Great for getting across quick updates, breaking news, and information. "Selling frosted brownies at the downtown farmers' market from 10:00 to 1:00. Weather's great. Come on down!"

5. **E-MAIL BLASTS**—Let people opt in to a mailing list and send them updates. Use these in the same way you use social media posts, but you can go into even more detail. Let people know what's going on.

6. **NEWSLETTERS**—Send them via e-mail or through the mail. Or if you know someone else who puts out a newsletter, see if you can do a guest post.

7.　**WEBSITE**—This is your domain. Make it great and keep it updated with everything you want the world to know about your business. See chapter 7 for more on creating and maintaining your website.

8.　**WORD OF MOUTH**—Don't ever underestimate the power of one friend telling another friend. It may be embarrassing sometimes to hear your mom bragging to her friends about what you're doing, but when it results in fans at your next art show or sales of your essential oils line, you'll be glad she spread the word.

9.　**FRIENDS' SOCIAL MEDIA**—You post something, then your friend reposts it, and so on and so on. Your friends may share a lot of your own contacts, but they surely have whole groups of people in their networks you don't know. A little friendly nudge and request to invite others to "like" your business can grow your fans exponentially.

10.　**OUTSIDE MEDIA**—It's not easy to get a TV morning show or a widely distributed magazine to do a whole spread on you and your business, but it can be done. Maybe you know someone who writes for an online publication and is always looking for new material. There are hundreds of websites that review products and tell the world about what's new. There's usually contact information readily available for you to open a line of communication. Take the first step and send a little note and photo with basic information and let them know where to find you for more. Do a little bit of homework first and let the media outlet know why your idea is particularly timely or newsworthy. Don't leave it to a blogger or news producer to understand the relevance of your business—spell it out in a pitch letter that explains why their readers would benefit from knowing about your product. Send a press release, which is a summary of who you are and what your news is, along with contact information so you can be reached. See the appendix for a sample press release.

"MY TOP PRIORITY IS FOR PEOPLE TO UNDERSTAND THAT THEY HAVE THE POWER TO CHANGE THINGS THEMSELVES."

—Aung San Suu Kyi, winner of the Nobel Peace Prize

CHAPTER 7

TECHNOLOGY

➤ THE WAVE OF THE PRESENT ◀

It sounds kind of silly to talk about technology like it's part of a science fiction novel, the wave of the future, and all that. The fact is, technology is part of our world today and it's part of every venture, no matter how low tech you may think you are. Technology can make us work faster and more efficiently, and it can help us communicate. That doesn't mean you need to drive yourself crazy or jump on every new trend in social networking or buy the newest computer to come out just because it's there. But consider what technology can do for you. Embrace it and let it make your life easier. Because wouldn't it be great to be a student, an entrepreneur, an athlete, an artist and still have time left over for some fun? Let technology speed things up where speeding up is possible, and carve out some extra time.

USE TECHNOLOGY FOR RESEARCH

You know when you get obsessed with a particular topic and you watch all the YouTube videos you can find about it? Well, that's research. Since you're already pursuing a business idea you love, doing research for your business will be just as interesting and fun! **KNOWLEDGE IS POWER.**

The great thing about this research is that you already have the skills to do it, thanks to every teacher who's ever assigned you a term paper or a big project. How did you get the information about World War I for that report? Where did you learn the difference between arthropods and their insect cousins? By doing research. Now you can use that skill for something in the real world.

ANOTHER KIND OF RESEARCH: FIRSTHAND DATA. That's the stuff that doesn't come from a book—it comes from asking real people what they think or what they like. It comes from informal surveys, from conversations, and from your observation of the world around you.

USE YOUR CROWD. Crowdsourcing is just getting information from your "crowd" to help you decide on a book title or figure out which logo to choose. It means putting a query out to your community and asking them to vote on choices you give them or make suggestions themselves. Post a picture of your tote bags and ask your crowd to suggest names for them. You could even offer a free bag to the person whose name you end up using to incentivize people to participate and make it more fun. That's one of the most important things we'll keep telling you in this book: just because you're in business, it doesn't mean you have to give up on fun. On the contrary, the more fun you make it to start, grow, and run your own enterprise, the better it will be.

ESTABLISH YOUR ONLINE PRESENCE

Even if you have the most old-school idea on the planet, you need an online presence to promote it, get fans, publish updates, and even sell right on your own website. Setting up a site is easy and inexpensive. First you need to purchase a domain name, which can be your business name or your own name with a .com or .net on the end. Using GoDaddy.com or Squarespace.com, you can search to see if the name you'd like to register is available and purchase it on the spot for around $10–$20 per year. Then you'll need to design your website, either by using templates provided by web design companies like Wix.com and Squrespace.com or by using tools provided by your web hosting company. If you're including a blog with your site, you'll find easy templates to publish through companies like Blogspot.com or WordPress.com.

Make sure you and your business are easy to find for anyone doing research and are appealing to anyone who comes across your website or postings. From Twitter and Snapchat to Tumblr and Facebook, there's a social site to fit every need. You don't have to be everywhere, but the more places you can have a presence, the more people who will know about your business. If you want to get really technical, you can even pay to have your website listed on a Google search or use Google Analytics to find out where social traffic is coming from.

MAKE TECHNOLOGY THE BUSINESS

PROJECTS BASED AROUND TECHNOLOGY ARE OUR FUTURE. We can do things from the comfort of our desks, in front of our computer screens, that we could never do in the past. That's both exciting—there are more opportunities than ever to create something—and challenging in its own ways. It can feel isolating to work alone at a computer. Technology is also fast moving, and sometimes it can feel daunting to keep up.

BLOGGING IS FUN. It's a great outlet for your thoughts, your observations, and your frustrations. And what if, after a while, you find that you have hundreds or even thousands of followers? Your blog is resonating with a consistent audience, which might mean you could field an advertiser or two. Or your six dozen blog entries might be the makings of a book. There can be serious money at stake, so keep an eye open to the business possibilities.

PEOPLE WHO UNDERSTAND TECHNOLOGY ARE ALWAYS NEEDED. Web designers, programmers, and quality assurance testers can offer consulting services to those who don't get technology at all. Even if technology doesn't form the backbone of your business, you will need to incorporate it into the way you run your company. From e-mail blasts to Skype conversations with business partners and buying supplies online, opportunities are endless.

BUT REMEMBER—TECHNOLOGY CAN'T DO EVERYTHING. There has to be a motivated soul behind it, pushing an idea or plan forward. Technology is a tool.

APPS

TODAY THERE ARE SO MANY USER-FRIENDLY WAYS TO BUILD AN APP, it can feel like everyone in town has an idea to create one. Depending on the type of business you have, it might be useful to have an app of your own. They can be used on the go, on a smartphone, all the time. They tend to work best for businesses in which your customers will need to book reservations (if you offer services or classes) or for business concepts built specifically for mobile use. This is where you need to have some intuition about your users and anticipate how they will find you and relate to your startup. An app isn't appropriate for every startup, and it's one more thing to build and monitor. But if it's right for you, there are abundant resources for building apps.

Juliette Brindak Blake worked with an outside company to develop an app for her Miss O and Friends tweens website.

JULIETTE

We worked on a Girl-to-Girl Wall app with Pinsight Media, a company owned by Sprint. It's a more accessible, popular form for girls and gives them the same socialization as on the web. They can download the app and still be connected to the database of Miss O, but they can access it from anywhere. We're working with a company that takes you in and upfronts the costs to build the app, and there's a revenue share until the money is paid back. They work with people at all different stages: For some it's their first thing ever. Others already have a following and an established brand. We had already created layouts of what we wanted the app to look like. We did a lot of legwork, so our costs are lower than someone new. But it's expensive to build a good, functioning app.

BUILDING A SIMPLE APP IS, WELL, SIMPLE. You can build a simple plug-in e-commerce app for little or no money. Apple, Android, and Blackberry all have OS developer programs for use on their smartphones, or if you have a handle on HTML coding, you can work with companies like Appcelerator or MotherApp, which allow you to build apps that can run on various platforms. Some charge a flat fee and others charge you monthly, depending on what you need the app to do. Once you get into more complicated functionality, that will dictate how much help you need building the next iteration of your app. Just be sure the value you get from your app will support the cost. In other words, don't pay a ton of money for someone to build you an app you don't really need.

E-MAIL

E-mail is still the most commonly used form of communication, especially in profes-sional spheres, where it's necessary to be businesslike and formal. That means watch your spelling, use a greeting and signature line, make sure you're being respectful to the person with whom you're communicating, and think before you send.

E-MAIL CAN BE TRICKY. On one hand, it's quick and accessible—but then again, that speed and haste can be problematic too.

It may seem like there are universal rules of e-mailing—or texting, for that matter—but when you really think about it, we all have our own individual rules. Some people think it's just fine to share personal and even shocking information via text. "We need to break up." "I'm in the intensive care unit." Other people think those are conversations best had in person, or at least over the phone.

LOL, TTYL, LMK may be de rigeur when you're texting a friend, but they may not be right when you're e-mailing someone you want to do business with. There are no hard rules when it comes to e-mailing. Ask yourself: will your recipient be offended if you don't start your e-mail with "Dear Jane?" Will she think it's rude if you respond to a question about startup cash in a one-line e-mail from your phone? The best way to avoid offending someone is to err on the side of caution, which means not being too terse. Until you really know the person you're dealing with, go a little overboard with a nice greeting, a complete message in whole sentences, and a signature from you. You can save the quickly dashed-off shorthand for when you've been working together awhile. A good rule of thumb is to see how the person you're e-mailing does it and follow suit. For example, if she capitalizes the first letter of every sentence and doesn't use abbreviations, you should do the same. If she sends one-word responses "sent from my iPhone," you can feel more free to be brief.

KEEP IN MIND that detecting a writer's tone through an e-mail can be difficult. If you think your pithy sarcastic humor gets conveyed though your e-mails, think again. If you're e-mailing someone you know well, your e-mail probably comes across in the manner intended. Your wink-wink diatribe meant to entertain might go awfully far awry if you're writing to a person who doesn't know your sense of humor. It's easy to offend people by being too brief, too casual, and too sarcastic.

WHEN TO USE E-MAIL

There was a time when any official business communication had to be signed, sealed, and delivered by mail. Now whole business contracts are executed electronically. You can write an entire book and never print it on paper. Writing your name at the bottom of a return e-mail is as legitimate as signing it in ink, as long as all parties agree.

As a general rule, e-mail is a fast, universally accepted way of communicating. You should always save e-mails that have anything to do with your business: agreements over how much you'll pay an employee, decisions about when something will be delivered, copies of contracts. You never know when you'll have to refer back to the time your supplier said you could have a bulk discount if you ordered more than 50 items.

E-COMMERCE

The convenience of being able to shop from your computer can make it tempting to do a little more shopping than you might if you had to drive someplace and pay cash. Now that you have your own growing venture, it's time to turn the tables and make it just as convenient for people to buy things from you.

YOU'LL HAVE TO DO A COUPLE OF BASIC THINGS TO GET STARTED. First, you'll need to have a website where people can do their shopping. Make your website easy to navigate and use, and include details and photos. See the appendix for more on web design.

DECIDE HOW YOU WILL ACCEPT PAYMENT. You can do anything from having someone mail you a check and shipping out your goods once you receive it to taking credit cards right on your website. If your product is available in an online store, you can link directly to that store. For example, if you've written a joke book that's available on Amazon.com, include a link to Amazon's website and let the buying begin.

CREDIT CARDS offer security and convenience for your customer and for you. You'll be able to sleep at night knowing that if someone has paid you by credit card, you will in fact be paid. No sitting around waiting to see if they'll remember to mail you a check. If you want to accept credit cards—Visa or MasterCard, for example—you'll first need to find what's called an "acquirer." That means you'll have a contract with a merchant bank or financial institution that will act as the go-between for you and your customer. Essentially that acquirer will pay you after your customer buys something from you and will then collect the money from your customer. Visa and MasterCard have lists of acquirers you can contact and will give you everything you need to get started.

Once you get the nitty-gritty paperwork and approvals done, you'll have a contract with Visa or MasterCard or Amex, and you'll pay a fee for each transaction they process for you, generally about 2% to 5% of the sales price. That fee will be a business expense for you, and the convenience and security of being able to get your money from a reputable company will make it worthwhile.

> ## WILDLY INAPPROPRIATE USES OF TECHNOLOGY YOU SHOULD AVOID
>
> * Using photos or videos of customers without their written consent
>
> * Stealing a smart, witty Tweet and pretending it's yours
>
> * Spamming everyone on your school's mailing list
>
> * Spreading negative rumors about a competitor

A PAYMENT SERVICE LIKE PAYPAL charges a percentage and a fee per transaction. The basic package lets you put the service's button on your website, which will link to their site, which is where payment actually takes place. PayPal and similar services offer other options, for a fee, that can give you more flexibility and convenience when it makes sense for your business.

JUST ONE MORE THING

THERE'S A LITTLE SOMETHING CALLED UPSELLING that you really need to know about. It means that when your customer has already shown serious interest in buying one thing, it may be a good time to interest them in adding something else. An impulse purchase—like that pack of gum by the cash register. You're waiting to check out and it's right there, very alluring and not too expensive, so why not? You can make that same strategy work in your favor as well. What's the best time to sell something to a prospective customer? When it feels painless and easy for them.

Restaurants do this all the time. "Would you like fries with that?" "Can I start you off with some of our fresh-squeezed lemonade?" You can do the same thing. When someone signs up for your cake baking class, ask if they'd like to buy an apron before the class, or a cookbook once the class is over. You already have a captive audience interested in your business—now it's your job as a business owner to do some selling. We know it may make you feel like the proverbial used-car salesperson, hawking anything and everything to make a buck. But you have integrity, and a good product, and you need profits to grow your business. Make a great product, offer a needed service, and you will be doing your customers a favor when they buy something from you.

SIMPLE WAYS TO UPSELL AND ADD ON PROFITS

* **ADD A CONVENIENCE:** For an extra dollar or two, offer gift wrapping.

* **GIVE A DISCOUNT FOR BUYING MORE THAN ONE:** You're selling one pair of custom-painted flip-flops for $10—offer two pairs for $16.

* **SELL TO YOUR CAPTIVE AUDIENCE:** You've just finished teaching a poetry class to kids—bundle up all the poems and publish a book you can sell to parents at the end.

* **SELL ADD-ONS:** You've used Groupon and sold 50 fitness classes. Now, when people sign up to redeem their Groupons, offer a towel or water bottle for sale.

* **REWARD CUSTOMER LOYALTY:** Print up a little punch card—for every hour of tech consulting you do for a customer, they get one punch. Twelve punches gets an hour on the house.

COMPANIES TO CHECK OUT

~~~~~~~~~~~~~~~~~~~~~~~~

WHEN YOU WANT TO ACCEPT PAYMENTS ONLINE

The first thing you need to do is make sure the payment system you choose works with your operating platform. In other words, if you are using an SaaS platform like Shopify, you'll have one payment system, and if you're using a self-hosted platform like Magento, you'll need something entirely different. There are three ways you can accept payment.

1. Have people pay through a form directly on your site, which sounds easy, but it's the least secure and probably not wise when you're starting out.

2. Redirect customers to a payment page that lives on someone else's site (like PayPal), which is safer but doesn't allow you to customize the experience to look like your own site.

3. Put the payment form on your site, designed however you'd like it to look, but have the payment transaction take place in the safety of a third-party payment site.

We like the third option the best, and here are some companies to check out that can help you set up a third-party payment site:

PAYPAL—paypal.com/home

AUTHORIZE.NET—authorize.net

PAYLINE DATA—paylinedata.com

STRIPE—stripe.com

"THE ONLY WAY TO DO SOMETHING IN-DEPTH IS TO WORK HARD. THE MOMENT YOU START BEING IN LOVE WITH WHAT YOU'RE DOING, AND THINKING IT'S BEAUTIFUL OR RICH, THEN YOU'RE IN DANGER."

—Miuccia Prada, fashion designer and businesswoman

CHAPTER 8

MARKETING

Y ou've created and set up your fantastic venture. You're cranking out eco-friendly faux leather bags or teaching speech and debate to elementary school kids. You've got enough songs written to take to your first open mic night, where a few industry pros are known to gather. Now it's time to spread the word about what you're doing to your potential customers.

DOES THE THOUGHT OF PUTTING YOURSELF OUT THERE MAKE YOU HYPER-VENTILATE? You're getting ready to put something you care deeply about out there for people to see, touch, love, or maybe even reject. It's scary. Every Boss has experienced that fear—you are not alone. And everyone has experienced rejection. No one likes it, but once you realize it happens to everyone and it's okay, you'll be ready to move forward. You will learn from it, and you have to let it make you more, not less, determined.

So take a deep breath and get familiar with one of the most basic concepts in launching your enterprise: marketing.

How do you get word of your product to the people likely to want it? You can stand on a street corner spinning a sign or shout through a megaphone, but there are more efficient ways to reach people in larger numbers. Ask people you know to make introductions to potential clients or others who might bring you some publicity. Not all those efforts will pan out, but if you keep it up, you'll see results.

That's how Alex Douwes and Nellie Morris got started when they were launching Purpose Generation.

◇◇

ALEX AND NELLIE

We made a list of our dream clients and went after three to five prospects at a time. We realized that "warm" leads were the most effective and reached out to any friend that might be able to orchestrate an introduction. We were fortunate enough to be connected with Denise Morrison, CEO of Campbell's Soup Company, who took a chance on us. She asked us to help her understand what Campbell's future consumers wanted and how the brand could remain relevant to this new audience. She saw something in us at the time, and Campell's remains a very important client for us today.

KICKING IT OLD SCHOOL

SOMETIMES THE BEST WAY TO MARKET IS BY WORD OF MOUTH. You tell your friend what you're working on and she tells her friend, and before you know it, a dozen interested customers are knocking on your door. Your first line of contact should be your own community.

Old-school tools like fliers, direct mail, e-mail blasts, business cards, and giveaways can get people's attention and don't cost much. Use your logo art, get the important information on there, and pass out your fliers and cards. Every coffee place in town has bulletin boards where local businesses can put up fliers letting people know about events and services. Ask if you can post your flier and be sure to design it with little tear-off strips at the bottom so people can rip one down and take your phone number with them.

Lots of stores will let you put a poster in their window, especially if it looks nice and has something to do with what they sell. For example, if your project is a 5K charity race, design a simple eye-catching poster with tear-off information sheets and walk up and down the retail block in your neighborhood asking who will display it. It won't take long to find someone willing if your poster is attractive and you walk in with a smile and a great attitude.

MAKE YOURSELF SEEN

USE YOUR PERSONAL SOCIAL MEDIA ACCOUNTS and the connections you already have to blog, tweet, and let people know about your business. These people are already interested in what you have to say, so they'll be excited to hear about your new venture.

Of course, you have to be careful about what you put out there for people to see and how often you post. You don't want people to get so sick of hearing about the new yoga video you made that they stop following you. Posting information that just sounds like self-promotional advertising ("Look at me, buy my stuff!") may not inspire people. If you're promoting a yoga video, post a 30-second video demonstrating how to do a pose, explaining how doing the pose three times a day will relieve stress. People will get a first-hand look at the kind of material they'll find when they buy your video, and it will be useful information for them to have. That's good, savvy marketing.

Use your existing network to reach a bigger network. People who know you may be happy to help. Guest blog for a friend, ask friends to repost your Pinterest photos, reach out to other bloggers and see if they'll link to your site from theirs. Just make sure that whatever you put out there has a purpose. It should relate back to your startup and push forward your goals.

LESSONS LEARNED
WHEN IT'S BETTER TO GO LOW TECH

* **When it accomplishes the same thing but costs less**

* **When your audience is more appreciative of a low-tech approach**

* **When it allows you to do something right away instead of taking lots of time to build infrastructure**

* **When the technology is untested and may have bugs to work out**

* **When you've exhausted high-tech solutions and you still want to do more**

* **Whenever low-tech will do the trick—don't overcomplicate things!**

Singer/songwriter Alyson Greenfield created a blog with a purpose—to win an audtion spot at the Lilith Fair music festival. Instead, it led to creating an indie music festival showcasing the amazingly talented women writing all sorts of creative music who didn't have a bigger platform to share their music. And thus was born the Tinderbox Music Festival.

◇◇◇

ALYSON

In 2010, Lilith Fair came back on the scene. I used to joke around and say if there was Lilith Fair now that I'm playing music, it would be great to be a part of it. So I started a blog called Dear Lilith Fair 2010 and started writing them letters. And wrote them songs and told them about all my feminist things and how I was a cheerleader in middle school and how weird that was, and I told them how I was on the board of the National Organization for Women and doing a young women's empowerment project. Well, I didn't play Lilith Fair, but I had another idea. That was the birth of Tinderbox. I had been thinking about starting a blog, but my friend said, "You need to have a purpose to your blog. You can't just have a blog, everyone has a blog." So I decided this lines up. I can have a blog about pitching myself to Lilith Fair. I was looking around at amazingly talented women who were writing all sorts of creative music, very innovative, different looking, and they don't have a bigger platform to share their music. And they weren't going to play Lilith Fair and I wasn't going to play Lilith Fair. I had done some showcases at South by Southwest and I realized I'm pretty good at this booking thing. I said, what if I just start an event that could showcase all these amazing women and it could be in Brooklyn?

FAKE IT 'TIL YOU MAKE IT

Sometimes you don't know the answer to a question, but you figure it out when your back's against the wall. Sometimes you don't know how to write a business plan when someone asks you to send one along, so you nod your head and promise to send it soon. Then you go home and research like crazy and ask everyone you can find for help, and then you write and send the business plan like you knew how to do it all along. That's just how it works—sometimes you have to say yes first and figure out how you're going to get it done after you leave the room.

So what if you've never pitched an idea before and your first potential client invites you to a pitch meeting?

Nellie and Alex realized they just had to prepare and jump into the deep end when they started Purpose Generation, a consulting firm to help companies better understand and reach millennials.

NELLIE

We lived by the motto "Fake it 'til you make it." We overprepared for every pitch, because we knew that we had to go above and beyond, given our limited track record. We practiced our pitches in front of every friend or family member who would listen, and we anticipated any question that might come up. Having a partner in this process was invaluable. I don't know how I would have done this by myself. We could finish each other's sentences and knew we always had each other's back, which gave us the additional confidence we needed to put ourselves out there.

Chelsea Siler of the Canadian Broadcasting Company/Radio Canada also jumped into the deep end when she was getting started.

◇◇◇

CHELSEA

When I was first starting out, I was a production assistant. I went on coffee runs, transcribed tape, did all the things nobody else wanted to do. Then I decided to take the next step. There was a new show being created. I was running the teleprompter, which is very stressful, for an audition of people who would potentially be on this show. I said, "I would like to be on this show." And I ended up being a correspondent. I always had a bit of self-doubt. I was supposed to be the PA and now I was on the show. But like they say, fake it 'til you make it.

I just kept asking, "You need a writer on this show, can I write a script? You need a producer, can I do it?" Sometimes they would say no and I'd be back on the coffee run. But then we went to LA and interviewed the actor Fred Dryer. I was the PA, but the producer had an allergy attack and couldn't stop sneezing. The person interviewing has to be silent, so the producer passed the paper of interview questions to me, and I interviewed Dryer. He ended up telling me a story he'd never shared details on publicly to the press, about some disagreement that happened on a show, and I went back with this tape that was the best we could have asked for.

From then on I was trusted to do these big celebrities. Had I not asked to be in that position, and had I not learned how to set up lights and how to be a really good camera assistant, I never would have been able to do it.

There's something to be said for jumping into the deep end before you really know how to swim. You're forced to figure things out and you don't miss an opportunity out of fear. Sometimes you can succeed precisely because you *don't* know everything. That means you aren't so cautious and you don't self-edit to the point that you've defeated yourself before you've even begun.

UNDERSTANDING CONSUMER BEHAVIOR

Watch what people do and make adjustments based on what you see. Sounds simple, right? It is. A consumer is anyone who buys anything, whether it's a service like web page design or an object like a screen-printed T-shirt. You are a consumer. You buy things you like.

START BY THINKING ABOUT YOUR OWN BEHAVIOR. What makes you more likely to buy something: Cool packaging? A sweet deal? Seeing it on someone you know who's a trendsetter? Not seeing anything else like it anywhere? A bulk discount? Exclusivity?

SEE WHAT PEOPLE AROUND YOU ARE DOING. Some people are early adopters, first to try out the new phone, first to have the new music system in their house. Then there are those who wait for the price to drop, for the bugs to get worked out, and for competition to make it better. And there are others still who wait for cheap knockoffs to pop up. What does *your* target market do?

ONCE YOU'VE FIGURED THAT OUT, you can come up with ways to deliver what they want. If you're targeting people who like to be the first to own something, you have to show them new stuff continually. If you want to appeal to the masses, keep your prices within reach.

TALK, TALK, TALK

Never underestimate the power of conversation. Or the blog you love to write. Yes, people do find out about things by searching the internet. That's not going to change. According to Google AdWords, searching online is the top way people get information about a product before they make a purchase. But do you know what comes behind as a very close second? Talking with friends and family. That means every conversation you have could end up as a sale down the line. It means that when your aunt asks how you are and what you're doing at your cousin's birthday party, instead of feeling like the last thing you want to do is talk about your venture, muster up some energy and gab away. Because that friend standing next to your aunt just might overhear you, and when you're getting to the part about the new ganache you're using in the wedding cakes you bake, she might announce that she's planning her daughter's wedding. She might hire you and after you dazzle everyone at the wedding, six more people might ask her who made the cake. Presto, you're in business, after one could-be-annoying conversation with a relative. You never know who might be listening.

Talk about what you're doing when you meet a friend for coffee and she asks how you are. Mention that you've been working hard on designing floral centerpieces for a holiday party. The person two tables over may be looking for a florist and you've just given yourself a personal pitch. Word of mouth starts with you.

We all trust our friends and family. If we want to try yoga, it's easy enough to ask a friend where she practices and go with her for your first session. If you're looking to get nail decals, you can probably think of someone who has the kind of nails you have in mind. Count on people to do the same for you. The next time someone needs a wedding cake, they'll probably ask a friend who baked hers. And you want to be the name she gives her friend.

Of course you can pay to have your business listed on Google or pay for other prime placements online. But do you need to do that? Probably not right at the beginning. The time may come when you'll need bigger strategies, and hopefully you'll have the income at that point to pay for them. But while you're getting yourself there, you can be sure that word of mouth is a powerful way to get the word out.

HOW NOT TO BE
AN ANNOYING MARKETER

THERE'S A TIME AND A PLACE FOR EVERYTHING. Choose an appropriate moment to mention your product. Don't market your business at a wedding right before the bride and groom say "I do." Don't call people during dinner and try to make a sale.

TAKE "NO" FOR AN ANSWER. Learn how to accept rejection calmly and graciously. If someone politely says no to you, accept it. Don't be a pest and hound that person daily for life. They may change their mind someday, but they definitely won't if you're a jerk.

DO RESEARCH BEFORE YOU TRY TO MAKE A SALE, and make sure your target customer is really a good bet. Does this customer really need your product? Have they bought one before? Can they afford it? Know the answers before you pitch.

BE NICE, polite, and not too pushy.

NEVER SPAM EVERYONE who happens to be on an unrelated mailing list you have. It will only annoy them.

LIMIT YOUR E-MAIL BLASTS to one per week—people hate spam.

GIVE PEOPLE THE CHOICE TO OPT OUT of receiving your e-mails or newsletters. (But hopefully they won't.)

"A SURPLUS OF EFFORT
COULD OVERCOME A DEFICIT
OF CONFIDENCE."

—Supreme Court Justice Sonia Sotomayor

CHAPTER 9

MASTERING SOCIAL MEDIA

Social media is already a part of everyone's daily existence, but there is a difference between using it to keep current by sending your friends photos and tweets and using it to promote your startup. There are good uses of social media and bad ones, and the trick is learning to distinguish between the two so you don't find yourself trending for the wrong reasons. The best social media campaigns go viral because they're thought-provoking or fun to watch, and if you can create something that generates shares and retweets while giving a shout-out to your business, you've cracked the social media code.

Not everything you put out to your friends and followers related to your startup has to be earth shattering, but it needs to matter. It needs to make someone take notice. That doesn't mean smothering people with an endless stream of posts on your every thought and whim. Save that for your personal feed. Limit posts about your business to one good captioned photo on Instagram or Facebook per day. Same goes for Twitter and Snapchat. Save multiple postings for something special: the ramp-up to the launch of your new song on iTunes, the countdown to your product's availability on store shelves or at a holiday boutique, the few days before your play is set to open. The countdown approach builds excitement, but you must use it sparingly.

People have a much greater tolerance for multiple postings if you include a contest or giveaway. It gives them an incentive to check back to see if they're one of the lucky winners of your soon-to-launch knitted skullcap with built-in headphones.

SIMPLIFY AND STREAMLINE YOUR SOCIAL MEDIA EFFORTS. You can populate your Facebook page with photos at the same time you're putting them on Instagram with one click and reach two potentially different audiences who only look at one or the other.

At its most basic, social media is a great, immediate way for you to crowdsource ideas and see what people think as well as share photos and news about what you're doing. It will help you stay current on trends and get almost instant feedback from fans and followers. Shares and likes will quickly give you great information about what you're doing right and what's catching the eye of customers you want to target. You can communicate about a new stationery design or an upcoming trunk show in a quick tweet, e-mail, or post, rather than having to rely on a traditional snail mailer that takes over a day to arrive. Plus it's free.

Keep an ear out for the next big thing. One day it's Instagram, the next day it's Snapchat. That doesn't mean you have to scurry around posting things everywhere in sight and hoping for popularity. On the contrary, pay attention and figure out where you'll get the right amount of attention for your business. Staying on the cutting edge often means more listening than doing.

Start by using the same social media sites you use to keep in touch with friends. Be assertive. Design a page with your new name and roll out your logo. You never know who might see a blast from you at just the right time to make a sale.

The best thing you can do is post something that gets reposted. Sometimes it's hard to dream up what that will be. If everyone knew how to go viral, everyone would. But think about the kinds of things you repost. Are they funny stories? Impromptu video clips? You know your friends and you know what they like. Even just saying "Forward this to your friends to help me launch my business" is a good way to start your word-of-mouth campaign.

Alex Douwes and Nellie Morris of Purpose Generation learned to be flexible about how they used social media.

◇◇

NELLIE AND ALEX

When we started, we wore formal attire and used corporate lingo in the hopes it would make us more credible in the eyes of our clients. But now that we've built a track record, we feel more comfortable showing off our personalities; in fact, we realized that our clients *expect* us to have more edge—that's what they hire us for, after all.

One challenge we face is that we're trying to cater to two very different audiences on social media: on the one hand, we have our clients, which are large corporates, and on the other hand we want to speak to millennials and potential tribe members. We have to find a happy medium and be respectful of the clients we represent, but we also understand that the purpose of social media is to show a more relatable side of yourself to the outside world by providing a window into your personal opinions and adventures. Every time we post pictures of ourselves traveling or at events, our engagement doubles or triples, so we're trying to get more comfortable sharing our personal stories on this platform.

DANGER AHEAD!

Of course, you have to be careful. Make sure what you put out into the world is really the right thing to be sharing. Never share intimate information or images. Do not provide your home address or phone number. Keep it professional.

Chelsea Siler, Canadian Broadcasting Company/Radio Canada, gives the long-term perspective.

◇◇

CHELSEA

If this tweet was on a billboard on the busiest highway with your face on it, would you be okay with it? I know anyone who is hiring me is going to go to my Instagram account, my Twitter account. I believe not tweeting that thing that is a little controversial is not going to change anything, but tweeting it could ruin everything. When you're in school, you're learning and developing and you're not thinking about when you're 33 and going to apply for that VP job. You're thinking about how you've had a really hard week of finals and you want to celebrate.

You have to understand how long things last online. So if you're going to put your name on something, it's going to last forever. Pictures still live forever. I don't like telling people to avoid social media because that's where communities live. But if you want to be a successful person in business and in life, there needs to be a filter in how you live online.

The Fe (Iron) Maidens, a high school robotics team, are mindful of the negative aspects of putting yourself out there on social media.

◇◇

CHARLOTTE, TEAM CAPTAIN

Our team is incredibly active on all forms of social media, including Facebook, Twitter, and Instagram. We use it to interact with other FIRST ("for recognitions of science and technology") teams; to keep our sponsor, members, and alumnae informed of our activities; and to help spread our message on women in STEM. As useful as social media can be, it can also be a very negative place. People can be much nastier online than they ever would be in person. And anything you put on the web will be there forever.

TMI AND OVERSHARING

SOCIAL MEDIA DOS AND DON'TS

DO LET FRIENDS, LIKERS, CIRCLES KNOW ABOUT SOMETHING NEW—a new jewelry design, a new place to buy your handbags, a website makeover. New things lead to new sales.

DON'T TELL PEOPLE EVERY TIME YOU CHANGE YOUR SHIRT or post what you had for breakfast. This works for some social media celebrities, but it's hard to get right, and if you annoy your followers, they may stop paying attention.

DO ANNOUNCE WHEN SOMETHING GREAT HAPPENS—you reached a milestone, sold your first 100,000 banana bread loaves, got your mustard on the shelves at Whole Foods. Let your customers, friends, and supporters share your success.

DON'T MAKE IT SOUND LIKE YOU'RE BRAGGING. Be gracious about your success. You're honored to have been chosen. You're fortunate to have this new opportunity. Humility is key.

DO INCLUDE PICTURES—use Instagram and Pinterest so you can show, not tell, what you're doing. Re-pins can do wonders for new sales.

LET SOCIAL MEDIA DO YOUR RESEARCH

Keep an eye and an ear out to what people are talking about, posting, "liking," and reposting. Use this to help mold your business ideas.

MAKE IT FUN. You can design a little chart or keep a running tally of how many friends have re-pinned a photo on Pinterest or reposted a video from Upworthy. Then do some thinking. See if you can figure out the magic ingredient that made it worthy of sending onward. Was it silly? Was it a parody of a hit song? Was it just a really great use of bananas and chocolate chips to make Halloween ghosts?

Then see if you can craft something yourself according to those conventions. Make your own social media campaign using clever, gorgeous photos or funny, catchy singing. Get out your cell phone and make a video about your business. Make it entertaining and friends will forward it on.

RESEARCH YOUR CUSTOMERS BY LOOKING AT REVIEWS online. Read reviews at sites like Yelp, Citysearch, and Amazon, places where users tell it exactly like they mean it. If a new gelato shop is churning out boring flavors, users are going to Yelp about it. If a rival has come up with the most swoon-worthy combination of chocolate and salted caramel ice cream, fans will be talking it up. Use that information to get clues about what people like, what they hate, and what they consider important. You'll find out tiny details you'd never dream up in a million years just by looking at a stack of reviews. Then use them to improve your business.

ASK FOR FEEDBACK DIRECTLY. Trying to decide whether your new logo is lost in the '90s? Ask your friends and followers. Looking for ideas for a great summer reading book? Just ask which ones everyone loves. Then use the information to make smart decisions about what to do. Direct research gives you real information, with the power to make you better in business.

IF IT'S NEWS, GET THE WORD OUT FAST

LET PEOPLE KNOW ABOUT SOMETHING NEW—a new clothing design, a new column on your blog, a buy-10-get-1 discount—via whatever social media your friends and customers are using to keep up with you. The immediacy of social media allows you to decide on the spur of the moment to have a fire sale on all of last year's designs. And if you let people know via social media, they can show up to your sale—today. You can find out that the local newspaper reviewed your new raspberry-vanilla cheesecake and let people know where to find it before the review has left the newsstands or migrated to the archives of the paper's website. Take advantage of social media's instancy.

Like anything whose upside is instant, immediate, and fast, there are pitfalls. Make sure you double- and triple-check what you're about to blast or tweet or send, before it goes out into the world forevermore. You can't un-ring that social network bell. Re-read before you send.

Remember to be consistent. If you commit to blogging or tweeting twice a day, don't quit. People get used to seeing regular posts and will begin to look for them. But don't bore them. Always have something new to share, even if it's just a new graphic or a current twist.

Chental-Song Bembry has sold more than 3,000 copies of The Honey Bunch Kids books and is working on a graphic novel and animated TV show based on her characters. She's a big believer in using social media to get the word out.

◇◇

CHENTAL-SONG

I'm on Facebook, Instagram, and Twitter. Using social media is all about nonstop promotion of your product. If you constantly put it out, eventually people will start to see it and you'll build a following.

I have used Google ads in the past, but I'm taking a break from paying for advertising right now, and I'm just promoting it myself and using a lot of hashtags on Instagram to help get the word out, because if people look at #art, they can see the pictures. You can't stop, because eventually people find you.

KEEP IT IN PERSPECTIVE

Why do we always warn you about keeping perspective, not letting things spiral out of control? Because it's human nature to keep plugging away at things we care about, sometimes to the exclusion of all else. Social media can be especially seductive and before you know it, you've become one with your screen.

We've all seen them: the irritating people who can't put down their phones while having a conversation with you. They may be sitting across from you at a restaurant, but their eyes are on their phones and their thumbs are madly at work, typing, scrolling, and keeping up with everything *but* what you're saying. Annoying, right?

You can stay on top of social media and use it to benefit your business without driving everyone around you mad. When you have your own business, there are two traps people generally fall into: having so much fun procrastinating and doing anything and everything to avoid actually working that nothing ever happens; or more commonly, working so hard around the clock that you forget there's such a thing as a workday. Your entire life becomes about work. But you need to keep everything in perspective.

Yes, you must work hard, and when you've started your own company, you are the one doing most of the work. But that doesn't mean you should alienate your family and friends because you're so caught up in growing your business that you are impossible to talk to. Put down the phone, close the laptop, shut off the e-reader, and have experiences. Be with people and talk to them without letting technology get in the way. It will be there for you later.

The beauty of technology is that it isn't constrained by time zones and waking hours. You can send off missives in the middle of the night if you feel like it. But the benefit of unplugging and living in the moment is that life is happening around you. You'll be privy to conversations and the hum of life, which is the very source of creativity a person needs when starting something new. You can't know what the world wants if you're blocking out the world looking at your phone. Put it down and just absorb the world around you. You'll be glad you did.

Gabrielle Jordan, who started Jewelz of Jordan when she was just 9 years old, has a slightly different take on social media in the context of the real world.

GABRIELLE

Social media is huge, especially nowadays. I grew up in a tech world, and even though it was before Instagram and Twitter, it was always around. I am not the best at social media personally, but I've been learning and working on it. It's so huge in business now, not just to reach youth, but to reach people on a large scale. You can network and brand and run a business on a laptop on your bed. It's making sure you post enough so people are able to see you but don't get annoyed by you, making sure every hashtag is designed to reach the right people to sell to, or the right people to hire you to speak. It's second only to being out in the real world. You don't have to stick with your state or your country—you can reach people throughout the entire world.

As young entrepreneurs, one of the things we have to balance is making sure we post as a professional but don't look too professional. Don't grow up too fast. Make sure to throw a dash of personal in there. I'm making sure I'm showing people I'm a young entrepreneur.

AGGREGATE!

TRY TO BE AS EFFICIENT AS POSSIBLE when using social media. Use programs like Postling, Spindex, Hootsuite, or Google Buzz, which can organize your social media into one location. Postling allows you to see where you're posting information and how it's being viewed. Hootsuite lets you set it up so you can decide where information should be shared and when. Google Buzz puts all the blog posts you like to read in one place so you don't have to click all over the web to find the blogs you follow.

THERE ARE ALSO APPS AND WEBSITES that help you consolidate RSS (Rich Site Summary) feeds into one place, run searches across multiple sites, and combine friends. Social networking and its aggregating services are changing by the minute, so it's nearly impossible to write something here that will be accurate six months from now. For your purposes as a new entrepreneur, just keep in mind that aggregators are out there and they can help you avoid having to search multiple places for what you want or can help you combine your feeds into one place. When that becomes useful for your project, you'll have plenty of help in getting organized.

"SUCCESS ISN'T ABOUT HOW
YOUR LIFE LOOKS TO OTHERS.
IT'S ABOUT HOW IT FEELS
TO YOU. WE REALIZED THAT
BEING SUCCESSFUL ISN'T
ABOUT BEING IMPRESSIVE,
IT'S ABOUT BEING INSPIRED.
THAT'S WHAT IT MEANS
TO BE TRUE TO YOURSELF."

—former First Lady Michelle Obama

CHAPTER 10

YOUR BUSINESS → SPACE ←

Your "business space" is not the physical location where you do your work. It's the larger, figurative marketplace where your business exists in the world; the other people, both colleagues and competitors, who populate that space; and the innovators who keep it changing and developing. We're talking about the people who work in your field. They are your people. They face challenges similar to the ones you're facing. They may have found solutions they're willing to share, or resources you just have to check out, or maybe they need help, just like you.

Seek them out so you can partner up, share ideas, commiserate, or pool resources. There's power in numbers.

WHERE ARE YOUR PEOPLE?

ONCE YOU HAVE YOUR TRUSTED GROUP OF CONFIDANTES, your sounding board, you'll have a handy cadre of people who can help you navigate the world where you will be selling. Sow how do you find them?

LOOK AROUND YOU. Do all the bakers you've met set up stalls at local farmers' markets when they're first starting out? Maybe this would be a good place for you to sell your artisanal biscuits. Look around at local art and craft fairs and see who is selling there. Look for ideas on how they set up their displays, how the best ones distinguish themselves from the masses, how you can learn from their best ideas. Don't forget to ask your colleagues what they do to drum up business. They can share their mistakes and you can share yours. Maybe you can all help each other avoid pitfalls in the future.

GET ONLINE. Have a look in the online space. Some (or all) of your community may be doing business online. For example, fan-fiction writers are usually only found online, writing and sharing with an online community. Find out.

EVALUATE THE MARKET AROUND YOU CONSTANTLY. If the last three art fairs where you've set up shop to sell clay mugs are saturated with pottery like yours, it's time to reassess. Does being in the company of similar startups give you a business boost because potential customers come to art fairs looking for pottery? Or are you noticing that people comparison-shop between you and your competitors three stalls over and you're losing out on potential sales? Maybe you'll need to do a trial run at a crafts fair where you're the only potter and compare that with how much you sell when you're one of many. Then decide on the best strategy.

SOMETIMES IT PAYS TO THINK LIKE A CONTRARIAN. If everyone's selling pottery at craft fairs, be different. Either sell something else or sell your pottery somewhere else. Go where your product has a better chance of standing out, or come up with a new idea that others haven't thought to try yet. Even if it's unproven, you can be the first to prove the concept. Never be afraid to go where no one has gone before.

KNOW YOUR COMPETITION

ALWAYS BE INNOVATING. The best way to do that is by knowing what other businesses in your space are doing. We're not telling you to look for ways to sabotage the other businesses in your field, but you do need to understand everything you can about what they're doing and how they're doing it. Sometimes this can be as easy as looking at their websites and simply observing. Do they use PayPal? Are they selling on Etsy? Do they blog every day or just once a week? Do they offer free samples or giveaways?

KEEP TRACK of this kind of information. List the companies you're following and describe the categories you're tracking. Maybe you're watching to see how often they update their blog or social media content, what they sell and when they introduce new products, where they're getting press coverage. Then spend some time thinking about how your business fits into this type of model. Does it make sense for you to be posting updates on social media daily? Should you display more photos than you have currently? If they're doing something great, you can incorporate it into your business.

THE BIGGEST DILEMMA you'll face when looking at your competitors is figuring out the balance between following along and finding your own path. If every event photographer whose work you've ever seen takes candid and posed photos, does it make sense for you to offer only candids? Customers may have come to expect both kinds of photos at their parties and may be disappointed if you take only candid shots that may not get four family members in the same photo. But if you've developed a signature style of candid photography that catches spontaneous moments better than others in the business, you'll give yourself a unique selling point, a reason to choose you over the jack-of-all-trades photographers. See how clients react. Keep a constant eye on your competitors so you can decide whether to do the same thing they're doing to stay current or whether you want to do things differently. There's no right answer.

TAKE CHANCES. Remember, fortune favors the bold. But do take calculated risks, not reckless ones.

YOUR WORKSPACE

YOU NEED TO SET UP SHOP SOMEWHERE. At first it will probably be at your kitchen table, in the garage, or in the spare bedroom of your house. It doesn't matter where your space is, but make sure it's your own. That means it should be a space dedicated to starting and growing your business, even if it's a single table in a corner where you can draw sketches and store supplies for your startup. Own that space, use it only for your business, and be protective of it. Don't shove your homework to the side of your desk and call it an office. Sooner or later, that homework will creep back in and your office may end up under a pile of binders and your comparative lit paper. Maybe you can find a couple of file cabinets in the garage, lay a piece of plywood on top, and make yourself a nice flat workspace with storage underneath. As your venture grows, your workspace will grow to accommodate it.

BE DISCIPLINED about the work you do when you're in your workspace—working at home takes focus. Set aside specific amounts of time each day to work on your business, like you're making an appointment or scheduling a sports practice. Even if you can devote an hour a day to coming up with ideas and getting your venture up and running, you'll find that in a short time, you'll have made a lot of progress.

CHOOSE A SPACE that allows you to be creative and to focus. If you can position your desk so you can look out a window, that might help you conjure up ideas. Find a good desk lamp that gives you plenty of light. If you're working on a computer, set up a separate folder for all work-related stuff. This will make life much easier later when it comes time to keep records, deal with money, and find what you need.

STOCK YOUR WORKSPACE with supplies and keep it organized. When you sit down to work, try not to get distracted by e-mails and posts from your friends. Sometimes it helps to shut down your e-mail account and turn off your phone while you're working. It's amazing how much more you can get done without those distractions.

SALES SPACE

If you aren't using solely e-commerce to sell what your startup produces (e-commerce includes putting your books on Amazon and your music on iTunes), you may need an actual brick-and-mortar place for people to come and buy what you're selling. If you're in a service business, this can be an outgrowth of your workspace, such as a conference room down the hall where you can hold a meeting, or it can be outside your workspace, in a public working co-op or even a coffee place where you can find a quiet corner for a pitch. But if your startup is producing something customers want to see and touch and feel, you might need to give them a place to do that.

KEEP IT SIMPLE AT FIRST. Maybe there are local street fairs where you can apply to set up a booth, or the farmers' market in your town may have room for you to set up shop on weekends. Remember that you can't just show up. You'll need a seller's permit and advance permission to sell in an open venue, but that's pretty easy to obtain. The laws vary from state to state, but generally selling requires you to complete an application and pay taxes on the taxable items you sell. Google "seller's permit" for the rules where you live.

SET UP SHOP IN SOMEONE ELSE'S STORE. You don't need to rent the entire place. You can ask the manager of a store that sells complementary items if they have a consignment program, which is a fancy way of saying they'll let you put your furniture or T-shirts in their store for a while to see if anyone would like to buy them. And if someone does, the store will split the profits with you. Some stores split these profits 50-50, but others might want to take as much as 70% of the selling price. Don't be afraid to negotiate, and make sure that you're pricing your items appropriately so that selling on consignment is still a good deal for you. If they really like what you're selling, they may offer to stock your goods on their shelves all the time.

A lot of small-business owners go with this tried-and-true method of finding places to sell: they go in person to the Whole Foods or the cute retail boutique down the road (remember that small-business owners often like to help other small-business owners) and ask if they'd like to carry their creations in their stores. Some may not have room and they'll tell you to come back later. Others may say yes right away, or offer a trial for a month or so. If your products sell, it's beneficial for those businesses as well—they're always looking for great new merchandise to attract more customers.

SHARING SPACE

AS YOU GROW, or if yours is the type of business that requires big machines or lots of space, you may find you need production facilities, an industrial kitchen, or a place with multiple sewing machines.

LOOK AROUND AT THE SHOPS IN YOUR NEIGHBORHOOD and see who's doing what. Do they have extra space? A desk in the back? Some equipment you could use? Some cities have organizations whose specific aim is to provide resources like screen-printing equipment or sewing machines to community members: do some research and see what might be available where you live. We've provided a handy guide in the appendix to organizations that might be able to provide this kind of help—or other support for young female entrepreneurs looking to get started with a business idea.

LOOK ON CRAIGSLIST and send out queries to your network to see who (or whose parent or friend) might have a space you can use for free (or in exchange for dog walking, babysitting, or something your business can provide). It may be that renting space is the best use of your dollars, and if so, go for it. But if you just need a place to get started, see if you can save on rental expenses until you have real revenues coming in—and you can spend that money on developing other aspects of your business.

TREND SPOTTING—YOU ARE POWERFUL

YOU KNOW WHO THEY ARE: the hip friends who always seem to spot trends first, to wear cool clothes before everyone else. Maybe you're lucky enough to be one of them. Most of us are not trendsetters—but that doesn't matter. Take note of which kids are the ones everyone looks to for fashion ideas—and study them! This doesn't apply just to clothes: there are trendsetters all around you in technology, food, arts, community service, services—watch what they're doing and use that to inspire your ideas.

GET INFORMATION FROM FORECASTS. This is much easier than it sounds. Researchers publish material online, and they send their information to newspapers and magazines. Trend forecasters want you to know they're right on the money if they've predicted accurately, so they'll put that information out there for you to find.

NITTY-GRITTY BUSINESS STUFF

AND HOW TO DEAL WITH IT

WHAT'S A DBA?

DBA stands for "doing business as," and it means that you are doing business under whatever name you've chosen. You have to register that name with your city or state/province so they can make everything official.

TAXES, SHMAXES

Yes, you have to pay them. No, the process doesn't have to cause a migraine. Once you are officially in business, the government will expect to hear from you. The good news is, when you're first starting out, taxes probably won't dent your profits very much. And until things get complex, you can likely file them yourself using a program like QuickBooks or TurboTax.

I'M NOT DRIVING, WHY DO I NEED A LICENSE?

Let the folks in your local government know who you are and what you're doing. They won't make life difficult for you, and they may even protect you. They need to know you're out there once you've officially set up your business, which means you need to update them yearly with statements of information and reports. Good news is almost all of it can be done online.

IPO?

Yes, hopefully one day. But not now. An IPO (initial public offering) happens when your business has grown enough that other people want in. They'll buy shares or tiny fractions of your business in exchange for giving you cash to grow even more. You'll lose part of your ownership, and you'll have other people holding you accountable for continued growth. It's not for everyone, and it's just one of many ways a business can grow.

THERE ARE SUBSCRIPTION SERVICES that will give you targeted research on a certain demographic, but there's so much information out there for free, you should be able to get everything you need. Check out wgsn.tumblr.com, trendhunter.com, and psfk.com. Even the paid services often offer a free demo or trial period, so take advantage and get a little information. Down the road, when your concept has become a moneymaker, you may be in a position to pay for trend-spotting services. Make note of the ones that do a good job.

DON'T BE AFRAID TO TRUST YOUR INSTINCTS, and do what you know. If you would read a blog about medieval witches, chances are your friends would too—and maybe others. If your venture involves engineering, follow everything that's happening at TechCrunch Disrupt and haunt the web for STEAM (science, technology, engineering, art, and mathematics) innovations.

REGISTERING A BUSINESS

MOST STATES OR PROVINCES HAVE A TAX EXEMPTION for businesses that earn less than a certain amount. California, for example, has a creative enterprises exemption if you earn less than a certain amount doing something creative. To access the rules for your state, go to the US Small Business Administration website at sba.gov and look at the business licensing and registration sections. While you're on the site, do a little exploring. The SBA has lots of useful information for small businesses. In Canada, go to CanadaBusiness.ca.

ALWAYS BE LEARNING

OVERPREPARE. Be the best-educated person in the room. Successful entrepreneurs never stop learning. Bosses are eager to understand the world around them, the larger marketplace that their business is part of, and the people whose needs their businesses are fulfilling. That is called context. To establish context you need to bone up on what other people are doing in fields similar to yours. Learn about their pricing, their clients, their business model. Google them, ask people you know about them, bookmark their blogs, follow their posts. If you're the kind of person who keeps all that information filed away in her head, go for it. If you like to make lists and use binders and tabs, keep track of all your data that way. If you're a fan of spreadsheets, use them. Just make sure you're compiling data whenever you can.

Say you're starting a nonprofit theater company. The best information about how to do business will come from other theater companies, both for-profit and not-for-profit. Some may charge the going rate for tickets, or mount shows based on donations only. Others may limit their productions to a single one-act festival per year and spend the rest of their time offering improv classes because that's the most lucrative model. If they've made mistakes along the way, learn from them. If they're doing something exceptionally well, take note. Look at theater companies' websites, visit their workspaces, see their productions, and interview the people running the show. Don't be afraid to ask for information. People love to help, and remember that you're all in the business because you love theater.

OF COURSE, EVERYTHING CHANGES BY THE MILLISECOND. Statistics that ring true today may be woefully out of date by next month. Stay on top of changes in your industry by remembering to check in periodically and do more research. Find out who the new kids on the block are. Who is doing something original? Maybe some business flamed out because of a bad strategy (none of our Bosses, of course). Stay current, and you'll find yourself answering questions about your industry before anyone even has a chance to ask.

WRITE A PLAN. All that research will come in handy if and when you write a business plan. A business plan is an extremely useful document that outlines the nature of your business and your vision for it. Writing a business plan is a good idea for any would-be Boss, and a necessity when you're looking to raise any money to further your venture. The more you know about other businesses in your field, the better job you can do of convincing investors that it makes sense to help you.

"IF YOU ARE SUCCESSFUL,
IT IS BECAUSE SOMEWHERE,
SOMETIME, SOMEONE GAVE
YOU A LIFE OR AN IDEA THAT
STARTED YOU IN THE RIGHT
DIRECTION. REMEMBER ALSO
THAT YOU ARE INDEBTED TO
LIFE UNTIL YOU HELP SOME
LESS FORTUNATE PERSON,
JUST AS YOU WERE HELPED."

—Melinda Gates, cofounder of the Bill & Melinda Gates Foundation

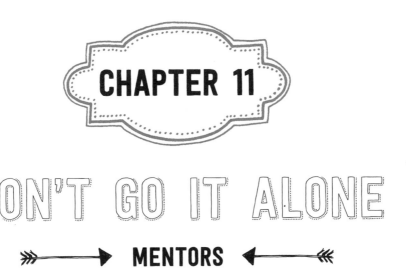

CHAPTER 11

DON'T GO IT ALONE

MENTORS

If you've seen *Shark Tank*, you know those Sharks have a lot of power to give new businesses money and awesome advice to help them grow. Not everyone is going to find their way onto network television to compete for the attention of a Shark, but that doesn't mean you're out of luck when it comes to mentoring. When you find yourself in need of advice—whether to bring on an employee, let's say, where to find them, what to pay—it's really useful to be able to turn to your mentor for advice. So make sure you have that person in place early on. The people who did just what you're doing a few years ago or even a few decades before you will have a lot of information to impart.

FIRST YOU NEED TO FIND THEM. Even a completely out-of-the-blue e-mail can begin a relationship with someone who could end up being your mentor. Check out the sample query letter in the appendix for some tips on getting the conversation started. Maybe this week is busy, but maybe next month there's time for a quick cup of coffee (your treat).

The idea of approaching someone cold may seem intimidating, but think about it: most of them are doing their jobs, same smattering of challenges every day, same people in their orbit of contacts. When a fresh young face pops up, filled with enthusiasm and lacking information, it gets everyone a little bit excited. Most of the time, no one asks people about what they do or how they got here—but people like to tell their stories once they know someone wants to listen. It gives them a chance to impart a little wisdom and maybe help another person out. Everyone wants to feel useful.

Priscilla Guo, who started the program TechY to teach computer programming skills to low-income students in New York City, emphasizes the importance of mentors in encouraging her to pursue her interest in computer technology.

PRISCILLA

I've benefited a lot in my life from role models, especially from female role models. I wouldn't be where I am today without the help of other women. I see that women are being discouraged from joining the technology field. Women are barely making the double digits in terms of percentage in the overall field. At Harvard, I serve as copresident of Women in Computer Science (WiCS), and under my leadership, we've doubled our numbers in our mentorship program. We have to encourage these kinds of supportive relationships between women to make sure they feel encouraged to pursue their interests and can share in each other's experiences.

MEET YOUR PEOPLE

WORKING ON A NEW VENTURE CAN SOMETIMES FEEL LONELY when you're first starting out. Launching something new takes a lot of heart, sweat, and work, and a lot of that work is the kind of stuff you do by yourself before you have the luxury of hiring helpers or getting out among your customers. The best thing you can do to make yourself feel like you're in good company is to reach out to others in your field. Look for blogs and websites that relate to your business, and comment freely on them or post questions and check back for responses. You'll immediately find that there are many others who share your concerns and can offer you advice.

SPEAKING OF ADVICE, seek out a group of informal advisers who can be your sounding board. These can be friends who are willing to read drafts of things you've written or to taste samples of your recipes. They can also be more formal mentors who sit with you once a month over coffee and offer you thoughts and advice on how your business is progressing.

COMMISERATING IS GOOD COMPANY. We all need informal sessions to blow off steam. You have friends who can be there for you when you're frustrated with life, but now you need a group specific to your work. They've done what you're doing now and lived to tell about it, even if there was complaining along the way. When you need someone to turn to, make sure it's someone who understands what you're going through.

One way to find those like-minded souls is to sign up for a class related to your project. You'll meet other people who share the

| **LESSONS LEARNED** |
| THE BENEFITS OF HAVING A MENTOR |

* **You don't have to reinvent the wheel.**

* **You can learn from someone else's mistakes.**

* **You'll have someone to commiserate with you about challenges.**

* **You'll never feel you're out there alone.**

* **There's wisdom in experience— your mentor can say, "If I knew then what I know now . . ."**

* **Your mentor may hire you someday.**

* **You'll be inspired to pay it forward and be a mentor to someone else.**

same interests, and who have varying levels of experience. If you're working on coding solutions in the company of a dozen others, you'll have a support network within reach if you hit a creative wall. You can also look for social opportunities—museum groups, fund-raising committees for nonprofits, sports groups—just make sure you find those like-minded souls. There will come a time when you'll be glad you did.

HOW TO FIND SUPPORT AND MENTORS

YOU KNOW PEOPLE. Your family and friends know people. Your teachers know people. And everyone you've ever interned for, worked for, or volunteered for knows people. That's your first circle of contact.

Start by letting people in your circle know you're looking for a mentor. Be specific about what you need: someone to give you advice on starting out or expanding, someone to give you a road map for a particular industry, someone to bounce ideas off of in a specific field, someone to come to periodically with questions. Then provide as many details as you can about your project or business. The more information your circle of contacts has, the better they can be at representing you to your potential mentor. In other words, don't just say, "I need a mentor," and end it at that. Better would be, "I'm looking for someone to answer questions about growing a stationery business from hand-cut and printed to letterpress printed. I know your friend Amy has been in business for years. Do you think she'd be willing to talk to me?" Then let your contact go to work trying to help.

Sometimes mentors turn up even when you haven't gone out looking for them. Your parents, in wanting to help and see your business thrive, may ask a friend to sit down and have a conversation with you. Take advantage of this new contact, who may have fabulous information and may end up helping you in ways you can't even imagine right now.

Mentors don't have to be a generation older than you to offer wisdom. Senior members of your school's robotics club or older students who've created their own

---

WHERE TO FIND A MENTOR

* The alumni association of your high school or college

* The alumni association of any schools your parents graduated from (high school or college)

* Directories of websites related to your business—often they list e-mail contact information

* Friends of your family who work in your field

* A boss at your summer job who knows you and wants to help

* Parents of your friends—think of them as people with jobs, not just as other people's parents

* Professional organizations related to your business—clubs, nonprofits

---

video games can offer a wealth of knowledge. So can a friend's older sister who turned her love of music into DJ gigs on weekends. Your school may even offer a formal mentorship program to match you with someone who can advise you.

Always call a contact who is offered up to you, even if you don't think it'll help. Maybe your dad's friend put you in touch with a colleague who is also struggling to launch a stationery business—but maybe she's a year into it and you're just starting out. She can offer you lots of experience and information.

You would be amazed at how often mentors are offered up and how infrequently they're actually called. Maybe you feel nervous or embarrassed, or maybe you're just really busy. But take a moment and realize how much you don't know. Then reach out to the nearest person who can give you information.

Mentors don't have to be heads of companies or elusive individuals who won't return your e-mails when you reach out for help. They can be friends of the family, bosses from summer jobs, teachers, or family members themselves. You just need someone in your corner.

Even though Neeka Mashouf is currently an engineering student who leads the battery unit of UC Berkeley's solar vehicle team, her first experience in seeking mentors was for a jewelry company she started with her sister at age 13.

◇◇◇

NEEKA

I have a twin sister, and when we were younger we wanted to be fashion designers. When we were 13, we started a jewelry company and marketed ourselves to fashion gurus. It was our own handmade crystal jewelry: pendants, necklaces.

At the time we were both big on watching YouTube gurus, so we tried to get in contact with them. We e-mailed a bunch, and the most famous ones didn't respond, but a step down from them, they did. Even though the top ones technically rejected us, we kept e-mailing people. On YouTube they had pretty huge followings and viewer bases.

THE 'RENTS

Yup, your parents deserve a word here. Of course you're working on your own project, and by the time you've gotten to the launching stage you may know a whole lot more about it than your parents do. But your parents have several decades of experience on you, even if the careers they have are completely different. Don't forget to look up every now and then and see what they might know about the situation. That problem you're agonizing over may be something they've experienced in their own fields. Lots of people deal with paying bills, ordering supplies, figuring out how to get office space, advertising. They just might know a thing or two that can help you.

Your parents might also end up being partners in your venture. Quite a few girl Bosses out there have started with incredible ideas, but they've needed a little advice on how to turn them into reality. Your dad is a great graphic artist? Bet he'll design your web page without charging you too much. Your mom is an accountant? Bet she knows the best program you can use to balance your books. Don't forget to ask the people nearest you when you have questions. They'll have your best interests at heart when they answer.

Chental-Song Bembry, who created The Honey Bunch Kids books, calls her mother her biggest mentor.

CHENTAL-SONG

My mom basically encouraged me to start The Honey Bunch kids, and to this day she's very involved in helping me build the brand. She's been my biggest mentor. I'm always learning from more people. The two animators I work with are people I can learn from because they've done it before.

No one in my family has owned a business before. My mom is a pharmaceutical sales rep and she's very competitive and tough. In sales you have to be able to keep going when people say no. Her personality and her experience as a saleswoman has helped me as an entrepreneur.

Deepika Bodapati, who with a partner created a portable blood-screening device, credits parents for mentoring and funding support.

◇◇

DEEPIKA

Our workspace is the kitchen table. We've always kept family involved. They've dedicated a lot to us. Because we've been keeping them along on the ride and we're very close to our families, they were really the only people we needed support from. We'd bounce ideas off everyone. They just knew. They said, "You guys do your thing. We're funding it." We're really lucky in that way to never have had that pressure. It would be a lot easier to say I'm going to be interning somewhere. But now I want it to work and I want to make sure we're working extra hard.

Juliette Brindak Blake, creator of Miss O and Friends, finds emotional support that keeps her going in something her dad always tells her.

◇◇

JULIETTE

There's this one piece of advice my dad always says to me. Whenever I don't think I can do something or I'm doubting myself, he'll say to me, "Do you believe in me?" And then he'll say, "Then believe me that I believe in you." And his saying that to me is always like okay, fine. It's always so heart-wrenching when he says that to me, but it does help me.

DON'T FORGET TO THANK THE PEOPLE WHO GOT YOU THERE

Yes, maybe those are the very same people we mentioned in the prior paragraph—your parents—but the advice should be extended to anyone who gave you a leg up. That includes friends who "like" you on Facebook or post positive reviews for you. Offering them a warm thank-you or a small gift makes them feel appreciated and makes them want to continue helping you. If your customers post reviews or check in on Foursquare, you can offer them incentives like discounts when they shop or free merchandise. Remember that merchandise with your logo on it can work as free advertising. If you give out free water bottles to the group of loyal friends who boost your YouTube views, you'll get exposure to new potential customers every time they whip out those water bottles at the gym.

THANK-YOU GIFTS AND INCENTIVES can be a great way to earn customer loyalty, but you don't have to extend your thanks in the form of a gift. A nice note is always appreciated. It shows you've gone to a little bit of effort to show your gratitude. It's the right thing to do, and it's also good business.

BE ETHICAL

Ethics are an important part of being a good person, but once you're a business owner, the stakes are even higher. You'll have more decisions to make, and your decisions will impact more people. For that reason, it's a good idea to think about your values and ethics in advance. What kind of products and ingredients will you use? How will you treat and compensate your employees? How can you give back to the community?

KNOW YOURSELF, KNOW WHAT LINES YOU WON'T CROSS, know what you expect from others, and don't settle. Business can get complicated by friendship and money, and can become especially dicey when both are in play at the same time. Friendships are important, and you should try to preserve them. If that means telling a friend you won't borrow money from her even if she's offering to fund a piece of your business, remind her that you want to stay friends and a few dollars isn't worth a potential fight later on. If a friend wants you to partner with her on a new venture but you know she tends to flake out on homework and you'll end up doing the lion's share of the work, do your best to avoid the potentially horrible partnership by giving your friend good reasons (time, a desire to do something else, or even just that you strongly believe it's not going to work for you) why you cannot commit. Don't give into pressure, only to end up regretting it later on. Be as honest as you can without hurting her feelings.

DON'T COMPROMISE ON THE THINGS THAT ARE IMPORTANT TO YOU. If you feel passionately about the ethical treatment of animals, don't buy from a supplier who has a reputation for being cruel, even if the price is half as much. If you want to print on recycled paper and use carbon offsets to make your business carbon neutral, do it. And let people know. Your ethical choices are part of your brand. Your customers, fans, friends, and anyone you come in contact with will respect your ethical decisions. Instead of hurting your bottom line because recycled products cost a bit more, your good-for-the-earth ethos may help your business because people will appreciate your taking a stand for the environment. Stay true to what you believe.

ETHICS APPLY TO COMMITMENTS AND AGREEMENTS, TOO. If you say you'll do something, follow through. If someone asks you to do something underhanded, feel good about turning them down. For example, a blogger might ask you for a hundred free headbands in exchange for writing a stellar review of them . . . hmmm, sounds like a bribe. On the other hand, if she asks for a couple in different styles so she can try them out before she writes her review, that's a normal part of doing business.

We know it's hard sometimes to keep your head above the drama. It can be tempting to tell someone who's writing an article about your business that you have more visits to your website than you actually have. But always be honest. If you hear a handful of people gossiping about someone else's company, it can be tempting to join in. But things you say have a way of taking on a life of their own or morphing into something even worse. It's better to change the subject.

Situations that force you to dig into your ethical reservoirs are also good opportunities to draw in your mentor. Get an objective view. Find someone to confide in and work out how to take the high road. Always take a moment and ask yourself to do what you know is right.

"THE VISION OF A CHAMPION
IS BENT OVER, DRENCHED
IN SWEAT, AT THE POINT OF
EXHAUSTION, WHEN NO ONE
ELSE IS LOOKING."

—Mia Hamm, professional soccer player and Olympic gold medalist

CHAPTER 12

MONEY STUFF

Starting something doesn't mean you have to go into debt or get a high-interest credit card and spend like crazy with no way of paying anything back. Begin by keeping your overhead as low as you can. You might have a picture in your mind of what a "real" startup looks like—a cool loft space in a brick building with big windows and an organic coffee roaster downstairs—and you might think you need that to make your venture seem legitimate. But before you shell out thousands of dollars in rent for a space you don't really need—yet—figure out how you can do what you do without spending too much money. Once you outgrow your home office or your garage or your kitchen table and your revenues are flowing in, you can find a great office. For now, see how low you can keep your overhead.

Alex Douwes and Nellie Morris were very conservative with their finances when they were starting their consulting firm Purpose Generation.

◇◇

NELLIE

We were working from my sister's apartment and had calculated that we could get by for a few months on our savings. We'd meet for breakfast before Alex's day job, and I relied on odd jobs here and there while teaching myself how to code.

ALEX

We were very thoughtful about how we set up our business. Traditional agencies pitch Fortune 500s for million-dollar contracts and hire big teams overnight to fulfill these contracts, only to have to lay them off again once the contract ends. We took the opposite approach and hired very slowly, while simultaneously building relationships with top freelance talent who met our quality standards and shared our values. Today, we are able to stay nimble and keep our overhead low by relying on a small team of general strategists with a very broad skill set and tapping into our pool of incredibly talented freelancers for engineers, developers, copywriters, and designers.

The media tends to focus on the outliers; the big failures as well as the young unicorns who drop out of college to start a company and sell it for hundreds of millions a year or two later. It's important to recognize that this is the exception, not the norm. We never expect to get anything we don't work our butts off for, and we always try to take calculated risks. We've never taken on any outside investors or big debt instruments, and we still work in coworking spaces because we travel a lot and like being flexible.

STARTUP CASH

This is where it all gets real: How do you find money to buy materials or equipment? How do you decide how much to spend? Where can you turn for that much-needed cash?

The answers are varied and depend on individual circumstances. We'll give general information here that you can tailor to your business needs, starting with how to figure out how much money you need in the first place. Try to be as minimalist as possible. If you don't need to travel to San Francisco in person to buy glass beads and can get them shipped for a few dollars, save that trip until you have many, many reasons to fly yourself there in person. If you can make a prototype of your solar radio with the funds you have on hand, think long and hard before shelling out more money to make three prototypes. Will having two more really give someone a better idea of how the radio works?

HOW MUCH MONEY DO YOU REALLY NEED per week to get your business started and to keep it running? Do as much as you can yourself: design your own web page, make your own business cards, design your own logo. That way you won't have to pay other people just yet. Labor is often one of the largest expenses business have, whether they're providing a service or a good, so you'll probably want to delay hiring any employees until it's absolutely necessary—wait until you have too many customers or too many orders coming in to handle them all yourself.

NOW USE YOUR ESTIMATES of how much money it takes to start and run your business and compare those with how much you think you can reasonably earn from your business. Ideally the amount you think you can earn will be greater (if not right away, then down the line) than the amount it costs to run the business. It's pretty common to be spending more money than you make at the beginning—so don't feel discouraged, as long as you can envision a time in the future when you'll be turning a profit.

START BY USING THE TEMPLATE we provide for earnings and expenses in the appendix. In the expenses column, list all the amounts you anticipate having to spend. In the earnings column, list the income you expect to earn, item by item. Eventually this sheet will shift from being estimates of expenses and earnings to records of the real thing, but it always helps to have an estimate in the beginning so you can see whether things are going according to plan or not.

BORROWING

One very effective way to get startup money is to borrow it, and there are many people and organizations willing to lend it on varying sets of terms. Banks charge interest. Some organizations ask for a share of future profits. Some people may give you a start out of the goodness of their hearts and only ask that you make them proud in return. What makes one source better than another?

LET'S START WITH YOUR PARENTS. It's easy to want to turn to them, and parents are often a great source of encouragement and funds. But just because you live with them doesn't mean you should treat your parents differently from any other lender. You should still work up some sort of agreement stating how much you're borrowing and the terms according to which you'll repay the loan. Be realistic. If you think it will take a year to repay what you borrowed, don't promise to get it back to your parents in a month. That will just make you feel like you couldn't deliver and it will make your parents feel like you weren't honest.

SET UP A REPAYMENT SCHEDULE THAT MAKES SENSE. Maybe you need $1,000 up front to rent an industrial kitchen, but you're catering three big parties in the next couple of weeks and you already know how much you expect to be paid. You can pay back the $1,000 in installments until you've paid back the entire amount. If you are paying interest, or a little bit extra for each dollar you borrow over time, factor that in as well.

DOES BORROWING FROM YOUR PARENTS MAKE YOU ANY LESS BOSS? Not at all. Does forgetting to repay the loan? Absolutely. So be a good borrower and repay the loan. Even if you've borrowed from your parents, you should still be responsible and adhere to whatever terms you set out—and communicate with them if there's a change in the situation.

THE SAME GOES FOR BORROWING FROM FRIENDS. If you do this, be very clear in your terms. Set out exactly how much you plan to borrow and when you will pay it back. The old warning about borrowing from family and friends is mainly based around the (hopefully unlikely) situation in which you borrow money and you can't repay it. Things can get tense. But if you follow through on your promises of when you'll repay the money and how much interest you'll pay, your lenders may be happy to loan you more money in the future if you need it. You'll be what's called "a good risk."

When Deepika Bodapati and her partner started Athelas, they were extremely cautious about borrowing money.

◇◇

DEEPIKA

Raising money is not an ancillary job. It's something we definitely had to learn. And then we were spending time on that rather than on actually moving forward on the technology. You want to raise money when you don't need it. We already are raising money.

Because we're students and we started with hacky science fair projects, we don't spend money. If people say, "You need this expensive machine," we say we'll do it this other way.

The first time we had an agreement for someone to put money in, we walked out of the building feeling nauseous as we drove home, so sick. When people commit that money, they expect it back . . . 10 times, 20 times. You don't think about it until you're in that position. Every investor will make you feel like you're on top of the world . . . and then, "Here are the terms."

We are mapping everything out very methodically. We have a week-by-week schedule we're keeping to, and at the end of this summer we want to raise a series A round [of funding], which is a seed round, which we never had to do before, because we did competitions and some venture capitalists gave us some money. But we know that at some point we need to raise money to scale up with institutional investors.

PROFITS!

You're selling something and earning some money for the first time. It's a great feeling and you should give yourself a high five for getting to this point. And after that all-too-brief moment of glory, it's time to get down to the big issue: what to do with that money.

We're talking about how your profits can continue to fuel your business. In essence, if your business is making more money than it's spending, you can be your own lender. You can use your profits to invest in equipment, supplies, marketing, salaries—whatever your business needs to do more and make more. In other words, you can grow bigger, reach more people, and hopefully be more profitable with that larger scale.

We're not saying you can't take any of your profits and use them to buy something fun. But you're the one who gets paid last. First you repay loans from other people, whether they're banks, parents, or organizations who fund startups. Then you invest in the future growth of your business, buying whatever supplies you need to keep going and growing. Then you pay yourself. If you do things in this order, you will keep your lenders happy, you'll keep your business running, and most likely, you'll have profits—money—for yourself.

MONEY LESSONS LEARNED FROM BOSSY GIRLS
WHO HAVE BEEN THERE

* People are more likely to lend you a second round of financing if you repay the first round on time as promised.

* People like to be part of something exciting—let them know your plans.

* Don't apologize for needing money—it means you're growing.

* Don't let money run your life—there's more to a successful business than money.

* You shouldn't feel pressured to disclose financial information just because someone asks.

* If you make a mistake, learn from it and move on.

BIG-TIME BORROWING

LET'S START WITH BANKS. While they can be a great source of small-business loans, dealing with them can also be complicated. You generally need a business plan and some collateral, or something of value, to guarantee your loan. When you buy a car, the bank agrees to give you a loan, and you can drive the car as long as you're diligent about making your monthly payments on time. If you stop paying, or default on your loan, the bank will take the car. Same goes with business loans. You need some proof that you'll be able to repay the loan. If your business owns equipment, that may be used as collateral. Or you may have to have someone else—a parent, possibly—cosign on the loan and vouch for your ability to repay it. In other words, they'll be on the hook if you don't pay. So be responsible.

BORROW MONEY FROM OTHER LENDERS. The US Small Business Administration (sba.gov) and CanadaBusiness.ca both have a wealth of information on applying for loans from microlenders, investment funds, or community organizations. These types of loans are generally best when you need substantial funds to buy equipment or ramp up production. When you are just starting out, it might be best to try to get what you need from more personal sources. For short-term loans, BusinessUSA (business.usa.gov) is a great starting point.

THE RULES OF BORROWING COUNT whether you're borrowing a few bucks from a friend or a few thousand from a bank: you need to pay the money back when you promised to do it, with interest if those are the terms. Don't borrow more than you think you can pay back. You'll be so much more likely to get offered a new source of growth funds when you need it if you pay back your lenders like a pro.

CROWDFUNDING

Just like you can crowdsource a name for your business by putting out a query on your social network, you can crowdsource startup cash as well. There are many established crowdfunding sites, and new ones are cropping up all the time. Some may take a percentage of the money you raise, and others may let you keep everything.

TAKE KICKSTARTER, for example. You set up a fund-raising end goal, say $15,000, to publish a first print run of a book you've written. You'll come up with small and large increments of money people can contribute to your project, along with little rewards you'll offer for each amount. Maybe you're willing to send a thank-you letter on fancy

---

YIKES! DOS AND DEFINITELY DON'TS
WHEN ASKING FOR STARTUP MONEY

DO be honest about how much money you need.

DON'T borrow money for your business and then post pictures of the expensive new bike you bought. Even if you didn't use your investors' money for the bike, it looks bad.

DON'T be afraid to ask for what you need.

DO pay the money back even if you haven't made a profit yet.

DON'T let money destroy your friendships.

DO separate business issues from personal issues.

PROS AND CONS OF BORROWING

MONEY SOURCE	RISK	REWARD	PRESSURES
You: money you've saved	It can take a while to save the startup cash you need.	You'll have the satisfaction of being in control.	It's your money at stake and you'd better spend wisely.
Investors, parents, bank, credit card	You'll be indebted to others. They may be critical of how you spend their money.	You'll be able to raise more money more quickly by relying on others.	You'll need to repay the money according to a schedule, often with interest. That means you'll have to generate enough funds to pay back your creditors.

stationery to anyone who donates $25. Then for a $35 contribution, you can offer the thank-you letter plus a bumper sticker. Maybe a $60 donation also gets you an e-book, and $100 gets you a signed hard copy. Offering little incentives is a good way to get people to make the jump to the next level of donor. Once you have everything set up, send out notifications via e-mail or social media to all your contacts letting them know about your campaign. Supporters have the option of donating with or without the incentives you've offered. On Kickstarter, if you don't reach your $15,000 goal, donors have the security of knowing their donations won't go toward a partially funded project. Only once you meet your goal of getting $15,000 in commitments from donors do you get all the funds.

OTHER SITES LIKE INDIEGOGO, CROWDRISE, AND GOFUNDME have their own versions of crowdfunding. Many of these other sites do allow projects to be partially funded, which might work better for you. And there are many others—shop around just like you'd shop for anything else and choose the one that best suits your project.

DON'T FORGET THAT YOU CAN COMBINE DIFFERENT SOURCES OF FUNDING. If you run a successful crowdfunding campaign, that's something you should tell a potential investor to prove that a lot of people are already on board with your idea and that you already have some seed money. People find safety in numbers, and if people are investing already, that's a good sign.

Here's how Neeka Mashouf created a successful campaign to raise money for the CalSol solar car project.

NEEKA

I designed, created, and marketed our crowdfunding project. I have always been interested in marketing, and part of that is knowing the right audience. You can't just throw out a campaign and expect people to donate. So I built a publicity campaign called 30 Days of CalSol. Every day I'd showcase a different member from our team and quote what the project means to them. Before, we were a faceless student group, but this allowed people to see the people on the team, the students, and what they were learning. The team was excited to get featured. Halfway through I realized after doing analytics that alumni were huge donors to the campaign, so I started targeting them specifically, saying, "If Cal has lasting impact on you, consider supporting us." It took three weeks to get to our goal and another week to get to our stretch goal, which was 125% of the original goal.

Crowdfunding isn't easy. It's not always just a matter of putting your project out there and watching the cash roll in.

Naama Raz-Yaseef found it challenging to use crowdfunding for starting a nonprofit program to bring irrigation to rural Zimbabwe crops in the drought months.

◇◇

NAAMA

It's very hard to crowdfund. I had no idea. There were times I thought maybe it would be easier to put the money down myself and get it over with. I deliberately started with a small ask amount, but that was also because I'd never done crowdfunding before. I do have intentions of doing more later, but I had no idea how difficult it is. It takes a lot of thinking, crafting. You need to build a community and ask people, Is this effective, and do you have ideas?

Building a campaign is fun. It's a lot of work, but it's fun and it doesn't have to be professional. I really like the concept of crowdfunding being a platform where nonprofessionals can bring their ideas. You can shoot a video with your own cell phone and that will be sufficient. Then fund-raising begins.

Getting money is really difficult. In the first several days I started with a very close network before my campaign aired. They contributed first so there would already be some money when it aired. Then I contacted a second radius of people and everybody contributed. It was great and very uplifting. Then I realized everybody close to me has contributed and I needed to reach people I don't know. That's the hard work.

PAYING IT FORWARD

Always remember all the people who helped you get off the ground, the ones who listened to your worries about whether you'd succeed, the ones who gave you great advice. Someday the time will come to pay it forward and do something for someone else. You could commit to mentoring someone less experienced, bringing her along as an intern,

ANATOMY OF A CROWDFUNDING CAMPAIGN

* **SHOW THE PROJECT WITH A VIDEO.** Let people know who you are—give them something to look at: a piece of the movie you're trying to get into festivals, a demonstration of your window-washing device. Put yourself in the video. Let people see you and understand how hard you've worked to get your project this far. Then ask for what you need.

* **BE CREATIVE ABOUT THE PERKS YOU CAN OFFER** at different levels of investment. A cool screen-printed T-shirt might encourage an investor to go up a level.

* **KEEP YOUR SUPPORTERS POSTED ON HOW YOUR PROJECT IS DOING,** how close you are to reaching your goal, how much time is left before your campaign ends. Don't be shy about sending your plea for support out a second or even third time to your friends and supporters who haven't contributed yet. Some of them may be intending to contribute, but they need another reminder.

* **SEND OUT THANK-YOUS AS SOON AS YOU GET DONATIONS.** Let people know how much you appreciate their help and support, even if it's just an e-mail. For a donor, there's nothing worse than feeling the recipient didn't even notice or care enough to say thanks. And remind your supporters once more what their funds have allowed you to do: go on tour with your band, finish your film, publish your book, produce your prototype. Be sure to provide your promised incentives promptly, too.

or answering her questions when she's just starting out. No matter how challenging being a Boss can be, you have valuable skills and information that can help someone else.

YOUR CONTRIBUTION CAN ALSO BE FINANCIAL. Kiva.org is a website that allows anyone to make small loans to borrowers around the world. You could offer up the sewing machine you bought but are only using one day a week to someone you know who wants to start her own business. You could have a company policy of giving a percentage of profits to a charity. Let people know you're doing it and make it part of your sales campaign so your customers will know *they're* giving back too, just by doing business with you.

KA-CHING—GET PAID

There are many services designed to make it easier for people to pay you. First and easiest is getting paid in cash. Cash is universal, and you can trust its value. But not everyone carries around much cash these days, so for expensive purchases, cash might not make sense.

Let's talk about an even more important aspect of cash: it's difficult to keep track of. Once you spend it, there's no record you ever had it. Unless you're really diligent about asking for receipts and keeping them filed away and labeled, you can go through a ton of money without any record of where it went.

Aside from cash, credit cards, debit cards, PayPal accounts, checks, and money orders provide an almost limitless array of choices. Credit and debit cards will be preferred by many of the people who will want to do business with you. The advantage of accepting credit cards is that you can be confident the credit card companies will pay you what you're owed in a timely manner. But what does all that efficiency cost you? Up to 3% of the sales price of whatever you've sold, and sometimes an annual fee or more. Different companies—Visa, MasterCard, American Express, Discover—have different terms, so you'll want to look into all of them. American Express is known for charging a bit more, but they also have great incentives for small businesses, so you have to weigh everything and decide what's best for you. Accepting credit card payments can be as easy as buying a tiny device that attaches to your phone and downloading an app.

IF YOU'D RATHER NOT DEAL WITH PLASTIC, you can make use of PayPal or PaySimple, or you can check the US Small Business Administration website at sba.gov or CanadaBusiness.ca for other payment choices that might work for you.

MONEY GOING OUT

As great as it is to have money coming in from sales, the reality is that you'll have **EXPENSES,** too, and you'll need a way to pay for them. If you have employees, they'll need to be compensated.

Some may be willing to work in exchange for a stake in the business you're creating together. If you hire someone to get the word out and do all the publicity for your company, your publicist may be incentivized to help you grow if she's guaranteed a bit of the proceeds.

If you can afford to pay someone for a dozen or so hours of work, there's no need to give up a piece of your business. Paying the people who work for you and the people who supply you with tools, equipment, and services means you may need to understand payroll services and vendor services. An accountant can make sure all this is handled correctly.

Paying your employees also signals to them that they're valued. Some businesses load up on unpaid interns, but that's not the work culture you want to create, and it's actually illegal in some places. Not to mention that asking employees to work for free wears thin over time. No one likes to feel taken advantage of.

BUDGETING FOR NOW AND THE FUTURE

This might not be as much fun as the creative side of your business, but in many ways it's even more important. You need to keep your finances organized so you have an idea of how much money is coming in, how much is going out, and how much you'll need for the future. You can accomplish all this with a basic spreadsheet (see appendix for a sample) that lists your income and expenses, and hopefully the two will even out by the end of a year. Of course, any money you have over and above your expenses counts as profit, and you have the choice of paying some or all of it to yourself as a salary, or investing some or all of it into growing your business. You don't need to put everything back into the business, but you should have an idea of big expenses that may be coming down the line so you can budget for them. If you need to buy a piece of equipment—a new laptop, some tools, rent on an office space—you'll need to account for those expenses and figure out when you'll have enough money to be able to pay for them.

You may be able to find funding for some big expenses, or borrow for them, but you can also get them the old-fashioned way: by saving up.

Deepika Bodapati entered several competitions to raise the startup money needed for her company, Athelas.

◇◇

DEEPIKA

When I came back in September for my senior year, we made the decision that if we don't make $15,000 by December, then we'll nix this. Tanay got the first $1,000 from a competition. We thought, *That is ten $100s—we can do so much with that.* We were so stingy about where we spent money.

A few months following that, I did two competitions at USC (winning the USC Stevens Most Innovative Award for $7,000 and the 4th annual Silicon Beach Awards Venture Competition for $25,000) and we had $32,000. For the Silicon Beach award, we were competing against PhD students. I was texting Tanay saying a crush of doctors had just rolled up and they're going to be presenting next to me. There's a dentist here who just invented a new orthodontia device. Well, we won the $25,000 at USC. I didn't know anyone in the audience. I had this fat check and I just went back to my dorm room.

PUT YOUR MONEY AWAY

Once you have money coming in you'll probably want to open a checking account and let a bank hold onto your hard-earned revenues. Most banks make a distinction between a regular savings or checking account for personal use and one you use for business. For one thing, they may give you different interest rates, a different number of checks you can write without being charged each month, and other helpful services like the ability to borrow for small business expenses that may come along—but they may also charge extra fees for business accounts because of these additional services. Have a conversation with the people at the bank and find out what they can offer you to help your new business. You don't necessarily need a mentor's help, but she might have good advice to offer about navigating the system at the bank.

The good thing about having your money in a bank account is that it will be harder for you to spend it frivolously. If you need to get out your checkbook each time you have a business expense, you'll be more careful about what you spend than if you're carrying around cash. But more importantly, you'll have a record of every dime you spend. That will be very helpful when it comes time to pay taxes or update your business plan.

ALWAYS HAVE A PAPER TRAIL

You need to keep good records of the money you earn and the money you spend. Credit cards and checking accounts can be handy for this, because they provide monthly and annual statements detailing everything you've spent, and you can keep track of your activity and charges online throughout the month. If you're 18, you can apply for a credit card that you'll use for only business expenses. But you should also collect receipts and keep them in a special place.

Organize your receipts into envelopes or files according to category, such as office supplies, web services, equipment—so you'll be able to find them when you need them. Receipts are especially important when you're paying with cash—otherwise you can quickly lose track of how much you've spent. Have a handy place to keep your receipts whenever you're out—a ziplock bag works just fine—and then file them away in your folder system when you come home.

Once things get a little more complicated, or if you just like to use computerized worksheets, you can turn to a whole host of programs to keep yourself organized. QuickBooks and other similar programs allow you to set up income-and-expense sheets and can keep track of every dollar you spend, whether you've written a check or paid cash. When your business is earning a profit, you'll begin paying taxes, and it will be enormously helpful to have everything organized through a bookkeeping program so you can figure out what you owe at the end of the year. Paying taxes may seem like a drag, but you can't owe taxes unless you're earning money, so having to pay them is actually a good thing—it means your business is thriving.

For more information on balance sheets, income-and-expense statements, and other business-related details, see the appendix.

WHAT'S AT STAKE

People talk sometimes about having a stake in a business—what that means is that they own a part of it. It could be a tiny fraction of 1% or it could be 49%. Ownership varies, but generally the greater part of a business an investor owns, the more input that person expects to have in the way things are done.

DO YOU HAVE TO GIVE SOMETHING UP WHEN YOU BRING IN INVESTORS? It depends. Some investors will want to influence how you're spending their investment and others will be more hands-off, so be sure you have everything spelled out clearly— who is responsible for what—in your terms sheet.

The new Jumpstart Our Business Startups (JOBS) Act allows for funding partners to have an equity stake in your business and eases some regulations that made it harder in the past. This is good news for startups in need of funding.

BUSINESS-Y TERMS
YOU SHOULD KNOW

REVENUES: Revenue is the amount of money your business brings in before you pay out any expenses like rent or stamps or paper or salaries (or even interest or taxes once your business gets big and your finances get more complicated).

NET INCOME: Also called earnings, this is a fancy term for profits, the amount of money you have left over after you pay expenses. This is money your business gets to keep, and you want to be profitable, if not at first, then eventually.

PRINCIPAL: The amount of money you originally borrowed.

INTEREST: This is a percentage of the money you borrowed that you need to pay your lender, generally monthly, in addition to the principal. You will also owe the amount you borrowed, and depending on how long it takes you to pay that money back, you'll owe more or less interest.

BALANCE SHEET: The place where you keep track of income and expenses. In a healthy business, the two equal each other and balance out.

THE BARTER SYSTEM

It may be that the last time you heard about the barter system was back in school when you memorized facts about trade, but the concept actually has a very useful function. Some of the best ways for a new business to get the goods and services it needs is by trading for them. In other words, if you can perform a piano concerto at your web designer neighbor's anniversary party and you need someone to set up your website, see if your neighbor is interested in a trade. If you are creating an online newspaper and you need someone to do marketing for you, think about skills you have that you can offer. Maybe 10 hours of babysitting the marketing company owner's eight-year-old will get you a marketing plan. Maybe another 10 hours will get you some business cards and 50 tweets about your business. Are you a website designer? Designing a company's website could be a good trade for a free month's rent at their office, coffee pods included. Be creative.

Remember that trading services is a cost-effective way to get what you need. Take advantage of the things you can do easily and quickly and trade them for the things that would take you forever. Do what you know how to do. Find people to help with the stuff that comes less easily to you—you'll discover that you're much more productive that way.

Deepika Bodapati traded her scientific knowledge for the laboratory space she needed for her science experiments.

DEEPIKA

I wanted to look into a problem I'd started at the school science fair: what's better, organic or nonorganic salad? I'd found that organic was worse—there were more contaminants. I wanted to go one step further but needed proper laboratory ventilation for my experiments.

At that time I was part of an organization called the Schmahl Science Workshops, which catered to low-income kids who wanted hands-on science experiments. I ended up trading my knowledge—they gave me space to work in and agreed to buy the chemicals I needed—and in exchange I did a lot of work for them.

"AS A LEADER, I AM TOUGH ON MYSELF AND I RAISE THE STANDARD FOR EVERYBODY; HOWEVER, I AM VERY CARING BECAUSE I WANT PEOPLE TO EXCEL AT WHAT THEY ARE DOING SO THAT THEY CAN ASPIRE TO BE ME IN THE FUTURE."

— Indra Nooyi, CEO of PepsiCo

CHAPTER 13

GROWING PAINS

Of course you want your business to grow. It's a sign of success, of progress. And it generally means the business is generating income, which is a good thing. You need to be profitable enough to keep going, even in a nonprofit endeavor. You can lose money for a while, but eventually, you'll need to bring in more than you lay out in order to have long-term prospects. Growth is the way to get yourself to higher profitability and more exposure. That leads to more customers or users and more income. And so on.

In a perfect world, your business would grow at an even trajectory, a little bit at a time, month by month, so you could prepare for expenses, challenges, and improvements down the line. In the real world, things tend to move in fits and starts, with some growth spurts that you expect after a period of investment and hard work and others you didn't anticipate. Sometimes business will be slow despite all your hard work. Don't read too much into it. Just keep going.

THERE'S ANOTHER ASPECT OF GROWTH: CHANGE. Sometimes you can plan for changes, and other times the changes sneak up on you and force you to cede ground or be creative to get to the next stage. Growth can be unpredictable. It can take the form of two steps forward, one step back, but it's also taking you to uncharted territory, which can be new, different, challenging, and great.

In starting Tinderbox Music Festival, Alyson Greenfield was faced with how to handle instant growth.

◇◇

ALYSON

I put myself in the position of creating something so big so fast that I didn't have the capital and the grounding to support it. I was still the person who did the business and did everything and was the face of it. I put myself in a position where everything was falling on my shoulders.

Juliette Brindak Blake found, for her Miss O and Friends social website for tween girls, growth wasn't always predictable.

◇◇

JULIETTE

We've been in business for a while now and it hasn't always been us making money and doing well and having a lot of girls coming to our site, so it's definitely something that's hard. I think a lot of people, when they're starting a company, they kind of have this idea that it happens overnight and that it's this instant success. It's a process and it's something you have to constantly work all the time on every day.

When she entered Stanford University and began to focus on her computer science studies, Niharika Bedekar found it hard to keep up with the demands of Power Up, the nonprofit organization that she'd founded while in high school to help girls deal with puberty.

◇◇

NIHARIKA

Freshman year I was able to keep up with PowerUp, but the next two years it was harder. I was trying to learn who I am as computer scientist. I was abroad in Berlin, working with a nonprofit that teaches refugees how to code so they're more likely to get a job and a housing permit. It's such a good process for them in terms of settlement in new country, and it was extremely fulfilling to use my tech knowledge in a real way.

It led to a rejuvenation of my enthusiasm for PowerUp. I'm so lucky to have this technical base, and the core of who I will always be is doing something with my work positively affecting people's lives. I am service-oriented and nonprofit-oriented. PowerUp is a distinct thing that might be difficult to connect with other skills in college, but as I think about work I want to be doing, I know how fulfilled I am when I do anything with PowerUp. Now I want to find ways do that.

WRITE A FIVE-YEAR PLAN

START BY LISTING YOUR GROWTH GOALS. Are there certain numbers you want to reach? Is there a dollar amount in sales you're aiming for? Do you hope to have a certain number of employees, or even just one person to help you get the work done? Think about your ideal scenario, the place you'd like to be in five years. Perhaps you'd like to be doing a little less of the sales and marketing yourself. Maybe you want some partners to share the financial part of the business and help in funding your growth. This is the time to think big, to imagine where you'd like your business to be someday. Don't limit yourself by being overly realistic. Your growth goals can include markets you'd like to enter, ways you can make your business more diverse, and the office space you hope to call home.

For example, if you're baking scones, maybe now you're selling them to three cafés per week, baking every batch yourself, and using the kitchen at home. Your goals could include renting industrial kitchen space, hiring a baker or two to crank those scones out, selling them in your own pop-up shop on weekends, and getting them into Whole Foods in five years. Lofty goals, but there's no reason you can't achieve them. You have to start by setting the goals, then break them down into steps you'll need to follow to get yourself there. You can divide your plan into one-year increments with an end point at the five-year mark, giving yourself smaller, more immediate goals that will help you get there.

START WITH BUDGETING THAT GROWTH. Find out how much rent you'll pay on an industrial kitchen space and figure out how many hours you'll need to use it. Calculate the cost of ingredients. Think about the wages you'd pay to your bakers. Consider what you might pay someone to do your sales and marketing if you're too busy to do it yourself. Decide what roles you plan to continue to take on yourself. This is the foundation of a business plan. Business plans are important for showing potential investors and clients that you know what you're doing and you're prepared for what's ahead—and they're useful for keeping you on track even if you're not showing it to anyone else yet. Check out the sample business plan in the appendix to see where to get started. You'll document your success so far, your costs, your profits, and you'll use those to estimate what your business could look like down the road. Investors will want to see that before they hand over their money. This kind of plan will allow you to finance your growth and reach your five-year goals.

GROWTH CAN ALSO SAVE YOU MONEY: SCALE IS KEY. If you can leverage (or average an expense across everything it funds) the cost of, say, a $20 paper cutter across 10 packages of letterpress stationery, then it costs $2 for each package in startup paper cutter costs. But if you can sell 100 packages of stationery cut by the same paper cutter, it only costs pennies per package. Sometimes growing bigger brings your expenses down, because many expenses are fixed no matter how small or big your business is. In other cases—like running a restaurant and needing to hire more employees as it expands—the more you grow, the more employees you'll need and the higher your labor costs will be.

When Debbie Fung started Yoga Tree, she discovered that certain expenses went down the more yoga studios she opened.

◇◇◇

DEBBIE

Our costs are split across five studios as opposed to one. We have an external planner to locate sites, a realtor to identify new real estate popping up, and we're working with regional managers in studios to see where people are coming from. In 2008 we picked up a second space. We had more classes geared toward a larger range of students because we quickly realized we had to scale the business. We couldn't be efficient and only run one boutique studio. It's the same amount of resources and labor costs. To get synergy in business and efficiency, there had to be a rollout model of two, three more stores.

DON'T FREAK IF YOU DON'T GET THERE ON DAY ONE

It can take more time than we'd like to reach our goals, especially because once we've attained one, we keep moving the bar higher. Sometimes your path will take you to a place where you're doing work for someone else in the interest of building your dream. Just stay focused on your goal and make every interaction an opportunity for learning and growth.

EVERYONE HEARS THE WORD *NO*. It's just part of putting yourself out there and aiming high. There will be roadblocks, but remember that someone turning you down just means that one person didn't fully understand the potential of your idea, or the timing wasn't right, or that person was in a bad mood. There could be a million reasons—and you'll never know what they are. Just tuck away whatever information you can glean from the experience and keep going. Don't let *no* deter you from doing what you intend to do.

Here is some Boss inspiration for when you hear no.

◇◇

CHENTAL-SONG BEMBRY (THE HONEY BUNCH KIDS)

I've had a lot of people say no. There are still times today when I think about stopping but there's a voice that says *keep going*.

I think having roadblocks makes the journey more interesting. In The Honey Bunch Kids there are always roadblocks. The goal of the kids is to survive middle school and stay friends. Then one character gets jealous of another character. Things that happen to the kids are things that happen to real kids in real life because I want kids to look at that and say, "I went through the same thing."

PRISCILLA GUO (NYC TECHY)

When you're working with big institutional forces and other obstacles, you can begin to find a way around them by creating small changes. Start small, test your assumptions, and adapt your ideas.

Believe in yourself. Everyone has the capability of being a change maker.

NEEKA MASHOUF (CALSOL)

The whole path I took, there was always an underlying notion or mentality of *I can do it*. All these solar technologies felt pretty far-fetched, but we are taking our own initiative to improve the world. If you're really passion-ate about the world, there's nothing stopping you. Why wouldn't it be you to solve that problem?

NAAMA RAZ-YASEEF (LAWRENCE BERKELEY NATIONAL LABORATORY)

One challenge is dealing with the no. I'm hearing no all the time. Or "You won't be able to do it." Even having days of no one donating is a no. Other entrepreneurs tell me to focus on the yes and eventually it works.

CHELSEA SILER (CANADIAN BROADCASTING COMPANY)

After volunteering at a TV show for a year, my supervisor was trying to help me get a part-time position on the show, but I didn't get the job. He understood that I had the work ethic, that I always showed up at five a.m. when I said I would, so he said, "There's this company that does production here, Pyramid Productions. Why don't you apply there?" I had an interview, and I thought it went well. I thought I meshed with them, but then I didn't hear from them for six months. At that time, I was working at the mall in addition to volunteering at the show. I really questioned myself a lot. Then, out of the blue, Pyramid called and said they had an opening. My résumé had been on file with them, and I'd made sure to follow up with an e-mail every three months or so, telling them I was still interested.

ADMIT YOU NEED HELP

It's not a shortcoming to admit you can't do it all yourself. It's a sign of growth when you need to hire people. It can be hard to give up control. After all, in the early days of a business, you're doing everything yourself. You're controlling the brand image, doing the marketing, getting out there and selling, and most important, you're creating the product. Once you get busier and your business grows robust, there just aren't enough hours in the day.

TAKE A HARD LOOK at all the hats you wear, all the parts of the business you work on daily. Make a list. Maybe some of it involves thinking and creating. Some may involve physically cranking out hammered silver necklaces or pints of homemade soup. Some may entail sitting at a computer and writing daily blog entries and other social media outreach. You're dealing with expenses. You're managing your money and budgeting for future costs. Start by prioritizing these jobs in order of your skills. No one is great at everything—you are better at some parts of your business that others. You also probably like certain parts more than others. You may love hand-screening T-shirts but hate doing the social media part of getting the word out. Or you may like making the T-shirt design, but the slogging through batches of dye is not your favorite part.

Decide which parts of the business you absolutely won't let out of your clutches and which parts you wouldn't mind having help with. Then begin pricing out the costs of finding help with those tasks. Decide how much you can afford by looking at how much time a particular job takes and how much of your time can be freed up for something better by delegating. If you can create 16 new T-shirt designs a week and your research shows there's a demand for more designs, you may want to spend more of your time designing. If you can pay someone hourly to do your social media marketing, and that translates into selling a lot more shirts, it's a good investment. Think about hiring people as a trade-off for growth. The more you can grow by hiring people, the more you'll be able to grow—and hire more people.

LESSONS LEARNED ABOUT GROWING BEYOND EMPLOYEE #1

* Some days aren't easy. And now there are witnesses.

* People don't always understand what you mean.

* Sometimes you have to say things more than once. Or even twice.

* Sometimes it feels like the people who are supposed to be helping you are actually making it harder.

* People make mistakes. And generally those things can be fixed.

* Treat your employees the way you'd like to be treated.

* Managing people takes time and effort—remember that it's a job in itself, and it can be difficult, too! It can also reveal your strengths and weaknesses as a manager.

* Having employees who do a good job feels like the weight of the world has been lifted off your shoulders.

* Having more mouths to feed—or people to pay—can feel stressful. Anticipate it.

* Growth is good, even when there are growing pains.

* Tomorrow is another day.

DON'T HIRE JUST ANYONE

Deciding that you need to hire people is just the first step—deciding who to hire is its own challenge. It might seem tempting to hire the first person willing to do the job, but take a beat and remember that the people you hire are supposed to make your life easier. If you say yes to someone out of desperation, you may end up having the worst of both worlds: an employee you have to pay (or even fire) plus just as much work as you had before (or more if you have to work double time to fix mistakes).

WHEN IT COMES TO FRIENDS, hiring them might seem like a no-brainer—and if the friend you want to hire has the skills you're looking for and the two of you have spent time together in intense situations before, great. But be honest. If you love your friend for her fashion savvy, her late-night advice, and her brain power when it comes to power studying for finals, make sure to stop and think about your friend as you'd view anyone who came to interview for the job. If you need someone for cutting and pasting photos on holiday cards and

> ## DANGER AHEAD! SIGNS YOU'RE GROWING OUT OF CONTROL
>
> **IS YOUR EGO BIGGER THAN YOUR BUSINESS?** If you're making bad business decisions just because you want to be the one who decides everything, rethink it!
>
> **ARE YOU MAKING BUSINESS DECISIONS** based on what other people tell you to do? Advice from others can be great, but don't let them steamroll you.
>
> **ARE YOU SELLING OUT?** Have you found yourself saying yes to things you know are not right for your business because someone is dangling money before your eyes?
>
> **ARE YOU REFERRING TO PEOPLE** as employee #13 or "the dishwasher" instead of by their names?
>
> **DO YOU SLEEP AT WORK,** work in your sleep, and . . . well, never mind, 'cause you're just not sleeping at all?
>
> **HAVE YOU SAID THE WORDS** "This isn't fun anymore" more than a couple of times?

helping produce big bulk orders of stationery, but you know your friend tends to skim over details and hates crafty projects, is she really the best hire? Ask yourself how you'll feel about her as an employee and a friend if she lets you down on the job. Is it worth risking your friendship? And is it worth potentially hurting your business when you could simply post an ad at a local school or online for the exact type of employee you need?

BY THE WAY, IT'S OKAY TO TURN SOMEONE DOWN IF IT'S NOT THE RIGHT FIT. Don't feel like you're being mean. You'll feel a lot worse when you have to fire that person for not being up to the task. Just remember to be polite and kind about it.

WORKING WITH FRIENDS AND FAMILY

Lots of people will be quick to say a very loud "Don't do it!" Friends and business don't mix, just like family and money. Keep them separate or you'll risk losing both. But working with friends or family isn't always a recipe for disaster. On the contrary, think about who really has your back: often it's the people closest to you. Many of our Bosses have hired friends and family, especially while they're still in school.

Not only did best friends Alex Douwes and Nellie Morris decide to work together when they formed Purpose Generation, they hired Nellie's sister Logan as well. It ended up being the perfect solution.

ALEX AND NELLIE

People often advise you *not* to start a company with your best friend. We decided to do it anyway and couldn't imagine it any other way. We can read each other's minds and have developed complementary skill sets over the years. We can go into a meeting knowing who will answer what question and own what part of the conversation.

We've also been criticized for bringing on a family member as our first hire. We thought about that decision a lot. Logically, we wanted to keep family and friends out of this, but the most important factor when growing our team of two was trust. There really wasn't anyone else we trusted more than Logan, Nellie's sister. She has had to put up with her fair share of challenges as our first guinea pig. However, because of our deep trust and respect for one another, she has always addressed concerns head-on, which has helped us grow tremendously as leaders and managers.

We've also made plenty of mistakes when it comes to hiring. Talent is probably one of the most important things to invest in and get right, especially on such a small team. We learned that it's impossible to prepare someone for the perils and privileges of working on such a small team, so we instituted a two-month trial with every new employee to make sure that it's the right fit for both parties.

Deepika Bodapati ended up starting her business, Athelas, with Tanay Tandon, a fellow regular on the science fair circuit.

DEEPIKA

From middle school to high school, a big thing to do was science fairs. One of the most competitive was the Silicon Valley science fair. I did it from middle school onward. As you move through it from 9th to 12th grade, there are fewer and fewer people who do it, and fewer and fewer girls. For the kids who stick through it, if you're good, you travel the circuit and have a camaraderie with the people you travel the circuit with. Tanay and I were each other's buddies throughout this whole process.

We always wanted to do something together. When we got to high school, Tanay was working at the Stanford Artificial Intelligence Lab. I moved into imaging and worked with Stanford's Multimodality Molecular Imaging Lab. I published a few papers on cancer markers, the imaging of pain receptors on a molecular level. I got a very deep education in that field, so as we were moving into college and Tanay approached me working on a problem, I started giving him feedback. He said, "You know more about this part of if it and I know more about that part of it, so let's just work together." It was a very organic meeting. As college started, we hit the ground running.

BE A GOOD BOSS

By now you know that when we talk about your employees, we're including you in the mix. You, as employee #1, are the one who sets the tone for anyone else you have working for you or with you. The way you behave and the way you treat other people lets people know about you and your business. If you are a relentless taskmaster who never allows for a coffee break or a smile in the middle of the day, you may get productivity initially from the harsh crack of your whip, but you'll find that over time, people stop responding to your autocratic nature.

Start by treating yourself well—and that means cutting yourself some slack. Back off on the harsh self-criticism. Take a moment to breathe and survey the business from a distance and assess where you are and where you'd like to go. You can be hardworking and driven without driving yourself insane. It's the example you should be setting for anyone who does business with you and anyone who works with you. You are not just the boss of you, you are also your own role model. Be the kind of Boss you admire. That will allow you to be a better boss to other people.

The Fe (Iron) Maidens robotics team has some good advice for easing up on your self-criticism.

◇◇

CHARLOTTE, TEAM CAPTAIN

When you are feeling less than confident, it's often good to look back and recognize everything you've already done, and then look ahead and see everything you can still do. It can often be best, when you are feeling insecure or anxious, to sit down and get to work; getting stuff done can often be the best confidence booster. And, of course, your friends can always help you.

WORK ON YOUR WEAKNESSES, WORK WITH YOUR STRENGTHS

Learning how to manage people is not easy. Being a boss is not the same as being a good boss. Some seem to be born with an innate sense of how to take charge of a group; others struggle at it. Some find it easy to speak in front of a group; others feel their throats contract when their voice is the only one in the room. Work *with* your strengths and work *on* your weaknesses. That means you should do what you know you're good at but also try to improve at the things that challenge you.

Another important thing to realize is that you don't do anything in a vacuum. In the same way your startup is an extension of yourself—your idea, your creativity, your brand—it's also an extension of the way you approach the world. The way you do one thing is the way you do everything. So if you know you're in beast mode when you put on skis, let that translate into the way you attack your sales pitch. If you are a champion debater, you'll be the most well-spoken person in the room during your pitch. Let the areas where you've accomplished a lot in your life already fuel the areas where you're just getting started.

Chelsea Siler brings the strengths gained from being an ultramarathoner into her job.

◇◇◇

CHELSEA

I got into trail running around my thirtieth birthday. I set a really ambitious goal to run the Canadian Death Race before that birthday. That year, I got into ultra running. I learned confidence, perseverance, learned not to let anyone tell me what I can or cannot do. I went on and did two 100-mile (160 km) races—including the prestigious Western States 100.

I always say I'm an ultra runner. The thing I do in my spare time relates so much to my job.

Find that thing you're passionate about. Your passion doesn't have to be your job. I work in broadcasting and marketing. It's a digital, cutting-edge service, and I could always be online if I didn't stop myself. But I get to go somewhere and put my phone away and run. Once you run over 30 hours into the night, that stack of paper and deadlines doesn't seem so important.

Living in Vancouver, everyone is a triathlete, everyone is a runner. Sometimes I feel intimidated around them, and I think, *I just do this in my spare time*. I have to remind myself: I ran 100 miles, I ran up that mountain. Each time I do a race, I feel more self-confident. I've stopped caring what other people think.

REMEMBER YOU'RE NOT ALONE

Let people help you. It sounds obvious and easy, but when you start something and it's your baby, it's hard to let other people take parts of it off your hands. What if they do it wrong? What if they take the business you've spent countless hours getting just right and take it in a direction you don't like? Here's where you have to breathe. Here is where you practice the art of patience and remind yourself that starting and running a business is a process. You didn't form your venture overnight, so the process of training people to help you with it won't be instantaneous either. That just means you should be realistic with your expectations and cut everyone—yourself included—a bit of slack.

YOU GET OUT WHAT YOU PUT IN

You need to take time to get things right. Put in the time it takes to train people to do things your way. It may feel like you're spending valuable time teaching when you could be spending that time doing, but remember the old proverb: If you give someone a fish, she'll eat for one meal. If you teach her to fish, she'll eat for a lifetime. Teach people working with you how you want them to do things and they'll be able to take the reins from there. Choose your employees carefully, spend a little time with them, then take a step back and let things unfold. Go back and make corrections if necessary. You'll find that if you've chosen people who understand your mission, you'll be able to train them in no time. They will probably surprise you and bring new ideas you never thought of. Welcome those ideas. Soon you'll have a team that can't be stopped.

BE GOOD TO YOUR EMPLOYEES

A happy boss can lead a happy startup. You need to take that goodwill you gained from being good to yourself and apply it to all the people who work for you. Remember, they are helping you further your idea and your creation. Even though they may be getting paid, they are spending their time helping you. Think about inexpensive things you can do to make your employees feel good about their jobs. Maybe you can buy lunch or treats for your employees once in a while. Make your workspace a fun and positive place to spend time. Letting someone work at home sometimes doesn't cost you a thing and may gain you higher productivity. Someone who appreciates the freedom to telecommute once in a while may repay the kindness by doing a bang-up job on the work—and remaining loyal to your company longer.

Being good to your employees doesn't only mean giving them perks. Think of your workplace as a second home. No one wants to live in a house where people scream at each other and tension is thick. No one wants to work at a place like that either. Do your best to keep any personal baggage out of the workplace, and let the only drama be waiting to hear if you've made a big sale. It seems obvious, but there are many bosses and employees out there who don't know where to put the boundary between their personal lives and their work lives. It creates an uncomfortable environment for everyone.

EIGHT MISTAKES
NEW MANAGERS MAKE

1. Trying to be everything to everyone

2. Forgetting to ask for help

3. Calling for meetings when independent working will accomplish more

4. Micromanaging employees

5. Feeling obligated to hire people you know are wrong

6. Feeling guilty about giving criticism

7. Working around the clock to fix every mistake yourself instead of correcting someone else's mistakes to save time in the future

8. Confusing business relationships with personal relationships

CREATE A CULTURE THAT REPRESENTS YOU

BE AWARE OF THE CULTURE YOU'RE CREATING. Think about companies you admire and try to emulate them. Do they have a ride-share service, a stocked fridge, or educational speakers? What kinds of policies and ideas would create a place that you would want to work?

If you like to collaborate around big conference room tables for six hours at a time and have everyone order in lunch, you are creating a different kind of culture than someone who likes to have everyone work at home and telecommute. If you do your best thinking on walks and you choose a workspace with windows that open for fresh air, you're creating a different culture than a business where everyone sits in low-walled cubicles and can see and hear everyone working around them. None of these are inherently good or bad models. Your business culture needs to represent you and the type of environment that makes you and the people you work with the most productive and happy.

THINK ABOUT HOW YOUR TEAM WORKS TOGETHER. Does everyone require peace and quiet to think and write? Do people need communal spaces to collaborate? Try to incorporate this type of efficiency into your work environment as well.

Your business culture is a combination of the physical office space you have—whether it's your garage or a swanky rented loft space—and less tangible aspects like

---

OUCH! SIGNS YOU'VE LOST TOUCH WITH WHAT YOUR BUSINESS IS ABOUT

* You don't return phone calls, texts, or e-mails to your friends and family. Because they're not potential revenue generators.

* You're rebranding and spending money on new logos just because you lost one sale.

* You don't care what kind of business you have, as long as it's profitable.

* You're spending more time on social media talking about your business than you are thinking about your business.

* You have a new idea and you're ready to trash all your hard work to pursue it.

* You don't remember why you started your company in the first place.

ethics and communication style. Some bosses hate to hear criticism of any kind. Maybe they feel like criticism cuts down the thing they are trying to create, or they view it as a form of disloyalty. Other bosses set regular meetings for feedback, always looking to fine-tune and adjust business practices based on what is working and what isn't. Think about how you feel about criticism. Does it make you feel insecure? It's pretty normal if it does, so maybe you don't want to hear it in person. Maybe you want to send out anonymous surveys from time to time. Try not to shy away from constructive feedback. It's very easy to grow nearsighted when we're working closely on a venture and forget to see it in context. Rely on people you trust to give you that perspective and to help you work out the kinks.

"WE NEED TO ACCEPT THAT
WE WON'T ALWAYS MAKE THE
RIGHT DECISIONS, THAT
WE'LL SCREW UP ROYALLY
SOMETIMES—UNDERSTANDING
THAT FAILURE IS NOT THE
OPPOSITE OF SUCCESS, IT'S
PART OF SUCCESS."

–Arianna Huffington, cofounder of The Huffington Post

CHAPTER 14

JUST ONE MORE THING

Taking big risks can lead to big rewards, but risk can also lead to failure. Everyone fails sometimes. It can happen in a quiet way, like not getting that big order you were hoping for. Or it can feel like a big public disaster, like having a trendy magazine review your ecoconscious cosmetics line and call it a bust. Surviving those setbacks and learning to thrive after they happen is an art. Perservere. Learn from every mistake.

If you think of failure as a learning experience or an opportunity, nothing is really a failure. View your setbacks as small potholes in the road rather than impossible cliffs. Think of it this way: if you try something 10 times and then quit, you'll never be able to say, "It took me eleven times, but then I got it right." Let failure be your motivation for doing it better the next time. Learn from it, think about it, then move past it. It's hard—but so is running a business, and you can do that.

So if you're going to fail, do it. Admit it happened and figure out what you need to do differently next time. All great minds have faced rejection. All great products have had bugs—some small and some disastrous—that had to be worked out. In lots of cases, a mistake is just a puzzle that has to be solved. Think of setbacks as challenges and fire up your brain to meet them head-on and find an even better solution.

NELLIE MORRIS AND ALEX DOUWES (PURPOSE GENERATION) ON FAILURE.

Don't be afraid of failure. We both took the approach that failure is a good thing. If it doesn't work, it just motivates you to figure out a different way. We ran into a lot of walls at the beginning and people who didn't believe in what we were doing. Fortunately we have families that were very supportive. They taught us to "try your hardest and never stop believing in yourself." It's important to us that our employees feel they can take risks.

Also, don't be too hard on yourself, and avoid the comparison syndrome. It's easy to focus on the people in the limelight who seemingly "have it all," but the truth is that they probably don't. A lot of it is show and tell. Besides, you have absolutely no control over their success; all you can control is where and how you choose to spend your energy and time. We've always been very stealthy and rarely promote ourselves or the business in a public forum. We believe the work should speak for itself. Delivering excellent outcomes for our clients is what makes it all worth it.

DEBBIE FUNG (YOGA TREE) ON TIMING.

There's never a right moment. Our motto is "Ready, fire, then aim." Fire first and refine it later. I don't think we should miss opportunities that are time-sensitive. Because our industry is very transitional—we're here to stay, but yoga is ongoing trend—we don't want to refine ourselves into a formula, because by that time, we might have already missed an opportunity.

BUSINESS IDEAS THAT EVOLVED FROM MISTAKES

FAILURE IS YOUR FRIEND

POST-IT NOTES—Spencer Silver was trying to make strong glue and ended up with the lightly sticky substance that allows paper to stick and then easily peel away.

TOLL HOUSE CHOCOLATE CHIP COOKIES—Ruth Wakefield, owner of the Toll House Inn, tried to substitute chocolate bits for baker's chocolate. Instead of getting chocolate cookies, she created the iconic chip-laden version.

SCOTCHGARD—Patsy Sherman was trying to make rubber that wouldn't break down when exposed to jet engine fuels and dropped the substance on her shoe. Over time, that spot stayed clean while the rest of her shoe got stained.

KELLOGG'S CORN FLAKES—John and Will Kellogg were trying to boil grain, but they left the pot on the stove for days, resulting in the stale cereal that became the crunchy corn flakes we know and love today.

YOUR INNER CRITIC

You've heard it many times. That little insidious voice whispering in your ear: *You're not smart enough. You don't have what it takes. You said something stupid. You just embarrassed yourself. Sure, you succeeded, but you're just fooling everyone.*

Your inner critic can do a real number on you.

WE ALL HAVE DOUBTS. It would be strange and dangerous to feel confident all the time. A certain amount of doubt is a reality check. It's a combination of humility and knowledge that none of us is fabulous 100 percent of the time. But that's where the doubt should end. Endless self-criticism is a whole other ball game. Even if you're just being self-deprecating when you say, "I'm such an idiot" or "All my ideas suck," it would be pretty damaging if someone else began to believe that were true. Or if you yourself were to start believing it.

DEBBIE FUNG (YOGA TREE) ON FEAR.

You need to find the courage to take action in spite of fear, doubt, and worry. The thing that holds us back the most is conquering self-fear. For me, I still deal with it on an ongoing basis. Every time I want to move ahead, there's a little voice that overanalyzes all the little things that can go wrong. It's still an ongoing struggle to turn that little voice down. You have to let it give you that sense of curiousness but not let it overrun you.

JULIETTE BRINDAK BLAKE (MISS O AND FRIENDS) ON PERSPECTIVE.

If I get a comment from a parent like "You really helped my daughter through this awful time in her life, thank you so much," I think, *Okay, this is why I'm doing this.* It puts it back into perspective for me, why I actually started this, and what the point was to start it and to be there for girls in middle school going through a hard time.

FILL YOURSELF WITH POSITIVE THOUGHTS. There's enough negativity out there to pummel you down regularly and keep your ego in check, so don't go around looking for it or, worse yet, create your own. Surround yourself with a network of positive role models and your own group of pals who regularly boost your self-esteem.

Send your inner critic into hiding. Rewrite the dialogue. Bloom. Change something about the world. And go kick some ass, Boss. Start today.

GOOD LUCK. YOU'VE GOT THIS.

"WELL-BEHAVED WOMEN SELDOM MAKE HISTORY."

—Laurel Thatcher Ulrich, historian and professor

APPENDIX

OTHER STUFF

In this section, we've included some resources that might come in handy for starting your business. Feel free to use these sample business plans and profit and loss statements as examples to help guide your planning or to show to potential clients and investors. We've also included a list of organizations that provide support and resources for young female entrepreneurs—everything you need to start working on your goals and become a Boss.

QUERY LETTER

A query letter is a tool for outreach. It can be used when a friend or colleague is referring you to someone new to get potential business or information or when you're contacting someone cold to find out if they're interested in meeting with you or hearing more about what you do. It can be sent as an e-mail attachment or via old-fashioned snail mail. Or you can put the letter right into the body of the e-mail.

ELEMENTS OF A QUERY LETTER

DATE

(unless you're putting your query in the body of the email)

DEAR _____ :

Find a name. (No "Dear Sir or Madam," no "To Whom It May Concern." Do a little research. Find out who will be reading your letter. Don't send it without a name.)

I AM _____ **AND THIS IS WHAT I DO.**

(Introduce yourself here. Here's where you describe who you are, explain who suggested you write to the recipient or how you found them, and explain what your business does and any successes you've had so far.)

I AM WRITING BECAUSE _____

_____

_____ .

(Now it's time to say what you want; how can this person help you? Be specific with your request. Do you need advice on something in particular? Do you want to show them your product?)

THIS IS WHAT I CAN DO FOR YOU—OR THE WORLD.

(Sell it. Your concept is great—explain how great and what your goal for it is.)

I WILL FOLLOW UP WITH A CALL IN _____ .

(Say when you'll get in contact to discuss how you can work together. And keep that promise.)

SINCERELY,

BOSS

E-MAIL

PHONE

WEBSITE

BUSINESS PLAN

A business plan lets prospective investors, partners, or owners of a space you might rent see a summary of who you are and what your business does. It includes financial and growth projections and information about any startup capital you have already. Any business plan should include the following sections:

1. **A SUMMARY OF WHO YOU ARE—** the person creating and running the business. Don't forget to mention why you are particularly well suited to be launching your business. Talk about your experiences and the successes you've had.

2. **A DESCRIPTION OF YOUR COMPANY—**what it makes, what it sells, what service it provides, and how you know there is a need for it.

3. **AN ANALYSIS OF THE OTHER BUSINESSES IN YOUR SPACE—**that is, businesses that do something similar and how well they are doing it. Don't feel the need to say that every other business doing what you plan to do is failing at it miserably. Investors like to see that you are working in an area where businesses *are* succeeding. Just make sure you point out what makes yours different and potentially more successful.

4. **WHO WILL BE RUNNING THE BUSINESS WITH YOU?** Will you have employees? Managers? Unpaid or paid helpers?

5. **GET INTO DETAIL ABOUT WHAT YOU WILL MAKE AND SELL.** Include specifics about ideas you have, including patents you may have already applied for and received. Discuss plans you have to keep your product current. How long is it likely to be useful without needing to be revised?

6. **HOW DO YOU PLAN TO ADVERTISE, MARKET AND FIND BUYERS FOR YOUR PRODUCT?** Don't forget to mention all your Twitter followers or social media friends. They are proof that you have influence over a large group and that you have a potential market for your product.

7. **THE MONEY—**here's where you talk about how much money you need to get your project off the ground and how much you may need later on to sustain it. Refer to this as "round one" and "round two" of financing. Don't be afraid to state what you need, but make sure you can account for how you'll use the money you raise.

8. **HOW LONG DO YOU THINK IT WILL TAKE UNTIL YOU'RE UP AND RUNNING AND MAKING A PROFIT?** Don't feel pressured to say you'll be profitable right away. Savvy investors know it takes awhile, and they are patient. The most important thing you can do is to give realistic expectations and then meet them. Write up a realistic timeline.

EXAMPLES

You can find many sample business plans online, and it will be worth it to research and read a number of them before you start. Visit sba.gov, CanadaBusiness.ca, or bplan.com (these are just a few of many sites) to get started. Business plans can go into vast detail and run dozens of pages long, but here is a sample of the simplest version.

BUSINESS PLAN FOR WELL, CALIFORNIA
A NATURAL BATH AND BODY PRODUCTS COMPANY

EXECUTIVE SUMMARY: Well, California is owned by Boss Extraordinaire, who learned about creating healthy, organic products through studying at a summer program at the Health Institute. She makes body lotions, soaps, bath gels, and lip balms out of organic products sourced from ethical growers in California. Organic, handmade bath and body products have grown in popularity and are carried in mainstream grocers as well as local health markets. Well, California has a website (insert website URL here), where it currently sells its products, and will begin selling at farmers' markets this year.

MISSION: Well, California manufactures and sells organic body products sourced from growers and suppliers in California in order to support the local economies of California. The products are gentle and safe for most skin types.

COMPANY OWNERSHIP: Well, California is fully owned by Boss Extraordinaire.

STARTUP SUMMARY: Well, California's startup costs consist of ingredients used to make bath and body products, rent on an industrial kitchen space, as well as bottles and labels for the finished goods. Well, California currently has $5,000 from a Kickstarter campaign, which will cover expenses to produce 5,000 bottles of lotion, the company's first signature product, and 5,000 units of its other products.

STARTUP EXPENSES

Website design and maintenance $500

Ingredients $3,000

Bottles and Labels. $1,000

Accounting/Legal $500

First Month's Rent $1,000

PRODUCTS

❋ Citrus lip balm ❋ Berry soap ❋ Citrus soap ❋ Berry body lotion
❋ Avocado body lotion ❋ Citrus body lotion ❋ Citrus bath gel ❋ Berry bath gel

MARKET ANALYSIS: Organic bath and body products experienced a steady 10%
yearly growth rate from 20xx to 20xx, increasing in 20xx–20xx to a 20% growth.
Customers are increasingly interested in using safe, natural products on their skin,
which corresponds with a growth in sales of organic foods in the same period.

The key is to offer healthy natural products with a unique, distinguishing feature.
Well, California, does this by:

  ❋ sourcing all ingredients locally from within California
  ❋ using excess crop production of avocados and citrus fruits
  ❋ ensuring top-quality ingredients

MARKETING STRATEGY

a) Sell products from website

b) Sell products at local farmers' markets and craft fairs

c) Sell products at established retail locations

SALES FORECAST

[You will detail the specifics of these sales with charts and graphics.]

a) Year 1: $10,000 in sales from website, based on current sales figures
[Include these figures.]

b) Year 2: $15,000 in sales from website and local markets

c) Years 3–5: $50,000 in sales from placement in retail locations

MANAGEMENT: [You will detail the expenses and salaries with charts.]
Boss Extraordinaire will handle production and packaging of products, website design, sales, and marketing in year 1.

a) Well, California will hire sales representatives to staff local markets in year 2.

b) Well, California will hire sales representatives and production staff in year 3.

FINANCIALS: Profit and Loss Statement [see below for a sample] and all projected financial numbers.

SPREADSHEET

A spreadsheet is a chart with columns for different pieces of information, all organized so you can see it in one place. You've probably used them in school, but this might be the first time you've needed one in real life. Excel is the big daddy of spreadsheet programs, and once you open a new sheet, you'll see columns you can label and fill in with information. You can even set up equations to take the information you put in your spreadsheet and calculate other information from it. A lot of spreadsheets can be really simple, though—the main benefit is that you can edit and change the information without losing any of it.

WELL, CALIFORNIA: MONTHLY FORECAST

PRODUCT		JAN 20XX	FEB 20XX	MAR 20XX	APR 20XX	MAY 20XX	JUN 20XX	TOTAL
Citrus lip balm	Price per unit	$2	$2	$2	$2	$2	$2	
	Units sold	50	52	55	57	60	70	344
	Revenue	$100	$104	$110	$114	$120	$140	**$688**

INCOME AND EXPENSES STATEMENT

YOU KEEP TWO CATEGORIES OF INFORMATION: money coming in and money going out (income and expenses). List everything you pay out as an expense: rent on an office, supplies, web hosting fees, paint, computers, wages—anything your business pays for.

Then list all the money coming in—money from sales, startup loans, grant money, donations—any funds you receive.

If things are going according to plan, the income and the expenses should be roughly the same. That means you shouldn't be spending more than you're earning.

In a real profit-and-loss statement, you want the income and expenses to balance out in the end. As the owner and chief employee, your own salary is an expense. So whatever extra money you'd have actually gets paid to you, so your profit and loss statement can zero out at the end. If your profits are higher, your salary might go up along with it.

HERE'S WHAT YOUR STATEMENT MIGHT LOOK LIKE:

YOUR BUSINESS NAME HERE

Income Statement for
January–December 20XX

REVENUES AND GAINS

Sales Revenues. $25,000

Interest Revenues $1,000

Total Revenues and Gains. . . . $26,000

EXPENSES AND LOSSES

Rent Expense $2,000

Employee Salaries $5,000

Office Supplies Expense $1,000

Startup Equipment Expense . . . $5,000

Marketing and Promotion $1,000

Meals and Entertainment $1,000

Total Expenses and Losses. . . $15,000

NET INCOME $11,000

PRESS RELEASE

A press release is a public declaration of news you want to share, framed in the way you want the world to know about it. It's basically just a blast of information with contact details so reporters, bloggers, or researchers can contact you for more. Always keep it to one page and use the elements in the sample press release shown below.

Contact: ANN BROWN
www.boss.com

FOR IMMEDIATE RELEASE Well, California eschews waste by using California's excess avocado crop in its new product line.

REDUCING WASTE AND REVITALIZING SKIN
Avocado body lotion soothes sunburn while keeping extra fruit out of landfills.

Well, California, a local, female-owned business is now in the business of doing good for the planet. After talking with California farmers who have a bumper crop of avocados this year, company founder Ann Brown realized she had a solution to the problem of potential waste. Her company will use excess crop production in its line of avocado body lotions, while giving a portion of the profits back to California charity organizations this year.

SUPPORTING LOCAL GROWERS
Well, California has been in business for three years, providing organic, natural bath and body products sourced from California farmers. "We're giving back to local growers while providing healthy products for our customers," says founder and CEO Ann Brown. The company has a line of soaps and bath gels in berry, citrus and avocado scents, all of which incorporate the benefits of the fruit oils they contain. They company also has a line of lip balms and its signature body lotion line, Essence by Well, California.

"I was going to throw away seventy pounds of avocados this week," said farmer Jane White. "When Ann Brown approached me and asked about our surplus, I realized it was a win-win for both of us. We will be in business for many years to come."

RESOURCES: PROGRAMS THAT HELP BOSSES GET AHEAD

There are many others online and locally.

USA

THE BOSS (BRINGING OUT SUCCESSFUL SISTERS) NETWORK

Networking organization that supports the development of female entrepreneurs.

thebossnetwork.org

CHIC CEO

Website dedicated to helping female entrepreneurs start businesses.

chic-ceo.com

FEMALE ENTREPRENEUR ASSOCIATION

Online hub to inspire women in business.

femaleentrepreneurassociation.com

THE GIRL EFFECT ACCELERATOR

Two-week program for startups that benefit girls in poverty.

girleffectaccelerator.com

GIRL UP

United Nations Foundation's adolescent girl empowerment campaign.

girlup.org

GIRLS GOING PLACES ENTREPRENEURSHIP PROGRAM

A Florida-based program and conference designed to help girls start businesses.

girlsgoingplaces-afg.com

GIRLS WHO CODE

Focused on closing the technology gender gap, the organization offers a summer immersion program to teach girls to code.

girlswhocode.com

GOOGLE FOR ENTREPRENEURS

Partners with entrepreneurs and builds communities where startups can grow.

googleforentrepreneurs.com

LEAN IN

Nonprofit network for women to support one another through mentorship and peer circles. Based on Sheryl Sandberg's best-selling book *Lean In: Women, Work, and the Will to Lead*.

leanin.org

NATIONAL ASSOCIATION OF WOMEN BUSINESS OWNERS

Membership organization that unites women business owners into a national network.

nawbo.org

NATIONAL CENTER FOR WOMEN & INFORMATION TECHNOLOGY

National network that works to increase diversity in technology.

ncwit.org

NFTE NATIONAL YOUTH ENTREPRENEURSHIP CHALLENGE

Network for Teaching Entrepreneurship's semester-long or year-long programs for young entrepreneurs to create a business plan and compete for national recognition.

nfte.com

POINTS OF LIGHT CIVIC ACCELERATOR

Investment fund and accelerator for nonprofit and for-profit civic ventures.

pointsoflight.org/civic-incubator/civic-accelerator

SAVOR THE SUCCESS

Membership organization for networking and mentorship among women business owners.

join.savorthesuccess.com

STARTUPCORPS

Philadelphia-based organization that gives teens entrepreneurship opportunities.

startupcorps.org

SHE OWNS IT

Web destination and support network for female entrepreneurs.

sheownsit.com

TECHCRUNCH

Preeminent source for technology news and information on startups, with events including the coveted Hackathon, Disrupt, and Startup Battlefield.

techcrunch.com

WOMEN IMPACTING PUBLIC POLICY

National nonpartisan public policy organization that advocates on behalf of women in business.

wipp.org

WOMEN-OWNED SMALL BUSINESS (WOSB) FEDERAL CONTRACT PROGRAM

Helps women-owned businesses compete for federal contracts.

sba.gov/contracting/government-contracting-programs/women-owned-small-businesses

WOMEN'S STARTUP LAB

Year-long founder development accelerator in Silicon Valley.

womenstartuplab.com

CANADA

CANADIAN ASSOCIATION OF WOMEN EXECUTIVES AND ENTREPRENEURS (CAWEE)

Provides opportunities to build your contact base, share resources, acquire referrals, and develop skills and knowledge that will help your business grow.

cawee.net

CANADIAN WOMEN IN TECHNOLOGY

A global forum for women professionals to connect with peers, share knowledge, promote research, collaborate, and seek suggestions and advice on career advancement and business growth in the technology sector.

cata.ca/Communities/new-communities.html

CANADIAN WOMEN'S BUSINESS NETWORK

Provides affordable, effective online advertising and relevant resources to assist small businesses.

cdnbizwomen.com

WOMEN IN BIZ NETWORK

Aims to increase the overall well-being and financial success of Canadian business women through mentorship, advocacy, and skill-building events.

womeninbiznetwork.com

CANADIAN WOMEN'S FOUNDATION

Empowers women and girls in Canada to move out of violence, out of poverty, and into confidence and leadership.

canadianwomen.org

WOMEN IN LEADERSHIP

Creates inspirational programs that bring women together in developing their leadership skills.

womeninleadership.ca

CANADA ONE

Provides information and resources about Canadian grant and loan programs for young entrepreneurs.

canadaone.com/magazine/loan_programs.html

WOMEN'S ENTERPRISE ORGANIZATIONS OF CANADA

An association of organizations that provide programs and services directly to women business owners in Canada.

weoc.ca

STARTUP CANADA

Celebrates and distinguishes outstanding achievement in advancing Canadian entrepreneurship.

startupaward.ca

FORUM FOR WOMEN ENTREPRENEURS (FWE)

Educates, energizes, and empowers all women, encouraging them to become successful entrepreneurs.

fwe.ca

WINSETT CENTRE

An action-oriented, nonprofit organization that aspires to recruit, retain, and advance women in science, engineering, trades, and technology (SETT).

winsett.ca

YOUNG WOMEN IN ENERGY

Aims to address the recognized need to increase female presence, development, and leadership in the energy industry.

youngwomeninenergy.com

FUTURPRENEUR CANADA

Provides financing, mentoring, and support tools to aspiring business owners aged 18 to 39.

futurpreneur.ca

WEB DESIGN

Of course, there are many companies that offer web design services. But when you're just starting out, you may want more of a DIY approach. Here are some avenues to explore:

GODADDY WEBSITE BUILDER: godaddy.com/websites/website-builder

GOOGLE WEB DESIGNER: google. com/webdesigner

SQUARESPACE: squarespace.com

WEEBLY: weebly.com

WIX: wix.com

PHOTO CREDITS

Niharika Bedekar: Ashley Overbeek

Deepika Bodapati: Vijay Sarathy

Fe Maidens: Erica Hill

Alyson Greenfield: Chantilly Waryck

Naama Raz-Yaseef: Gayle Anonuevo

Chelsea Siler: Wendy D.

INDEX

STACY KRAVETZ is a journalist, author, TV scriptwriter, and entrepreneur based in Los Angeles. She is the author of several books, including *Welcome to the Real World: You've Got an Education, Now Get a Life!*; *The Dating Race: An Undercover Report from the Frontlines of Modern Romance*; *Keep Your Frenemies Close*; and *Girl Boss: Running the Show Like the Big Chicks*.